KU-875-003

RAILWAY ACROSS THE EQUATOR
—THE STORY OF THE EAST AFRICAN LINE—

MOHAMED AMIN · DUNCAN WILLETTS · ALASTAIR MATHESON

THE BODLEY HEAD
LONDON

Acknowledgements:

The publishers wish to thank Mr Hugh Ballantyne for the use of his
pictures on Pages 6, 22, 154, 157, 165, 183, 184, 186, 187, 188 and 189; Mr
Colin Garratt for his pictures on Pages 12, 14, 52/53 and the back cover; and
Kenya Railways for providing many historical black and white pictures
from their archives. We also wish to thank Kenya Railways and Uganda
Railways for their help and hospitality without which this book would not
have been possible.

First published 1986 by The Bodley Head Ltd, 30 Bedford Square, London
WCIB 3RP

© Camerapix 1986

British Library Cataloguing in Publication Data

Amin, Mohamed
  Railway across the Equator: The East
African Lines
    1. Railroads – Africa, East – History
    I. Title II. Matheson, Alastair
III. Willetts, Duncan
    385'.09676   HE3418.5

  ISBN 0-370-30774-7

This book was designed and produced by Camerapix Publishers
International, P.O. Box 45048, Nairobi, Kenya

Written by Alastair Matheson

Edited by Brian Tetley

Design: Craig Dodd

Typeset: Nazma Mohamed

All rights reserved. No part of this publication may be reproduced, stored
in a retrieval system, or transmitted in any form, or by any means,
electronic, mechanical, photocopying, recording or otherwise, without
permission in writing from Camerapix Publishers International.

Printed by Mandarin Offset Marketing (HK) Ltd.

CONTENTS

Half-title: Changing the hoop — single-line working at Kenya Railways' Equator Station.

Title: Kenya Railways' passenger express crossing Athi Plains, near Nairobi.

Contents: Down 'sleeper' from Nairobi crossing Makupa Causeway, Mombasa island. Pillars in foreground supported original Salisbury Bridge.

Overleaf: 'Mountain Class' Beyer-Garratt hauling upcountry freight alongside Nairobi National Park.

Following Pages: Light goods train crossing lattice girder bridge on Nanyuki branch line.

Children wave farewell as crowded Uganda Railways' passenger train in 1980s livery pulls out of Kampala bound for Kasese.

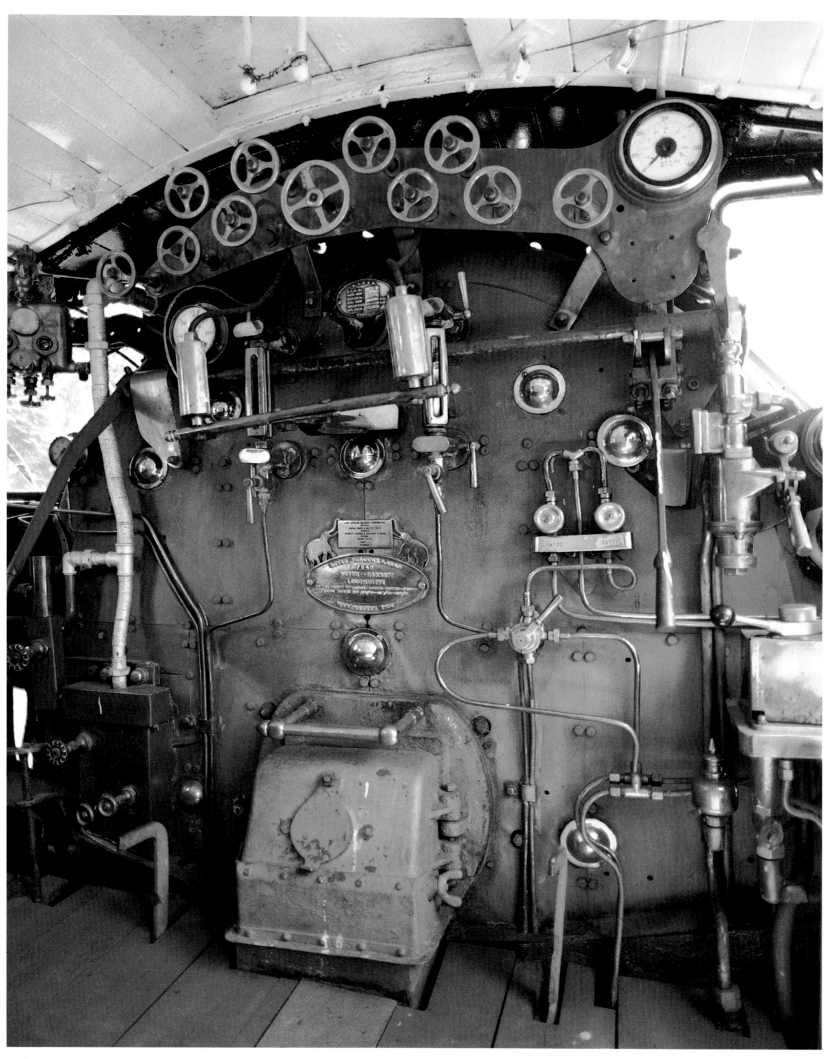

Left: Scene from the past. Veteran '30 Class' loco from the North British Works in the United Kingdom hauling a train of oil tankers.

Above: Gleaming brasswork on footplate of 'Mount Gelai' one of the articulated '59 Class' of Garratts — maintained by the same crew for most of its working life until its withdrawal at the end of the '70s.

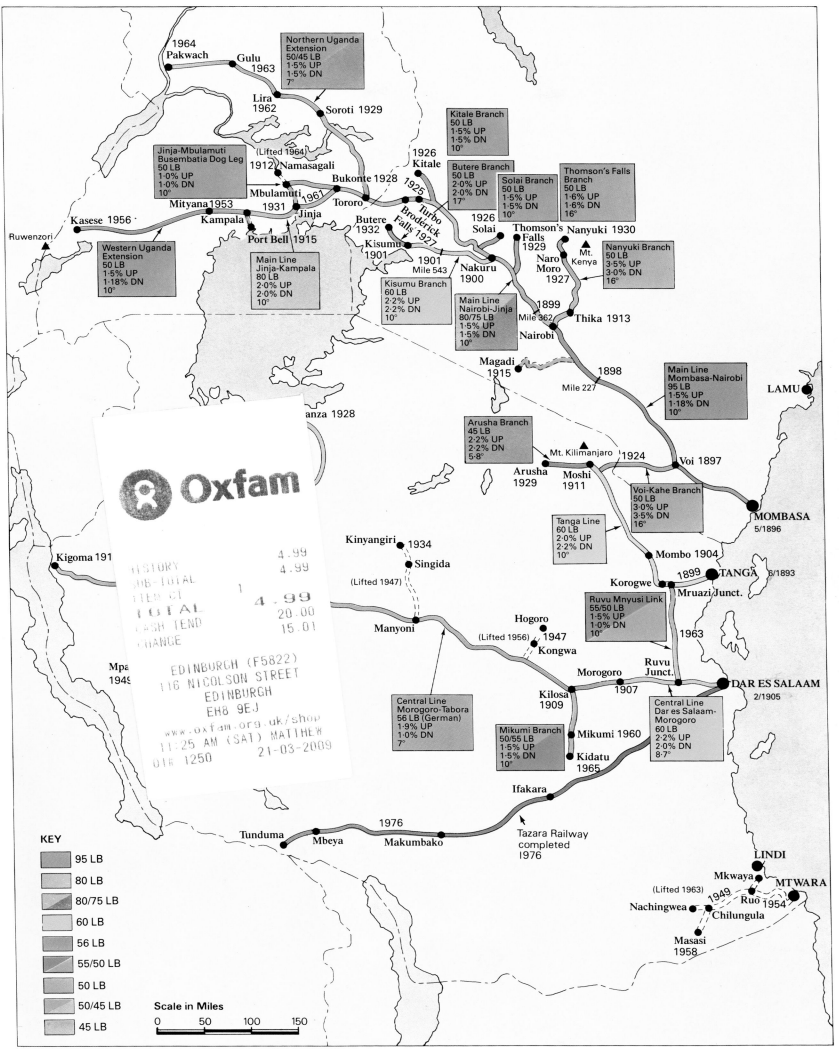

1964 Pakwach
Gulu 1963
Lira 1962
Soroti 1929

Northern Uganda
Extension
50/45 LB
1·5% UP
1·5% DN
7°

Kitale Branch
50 LB
1·5% UP
1·5% DN
10°

Jinja-Mbulamuti
Busembatia Dog Leg
50 LB
1·0% UP
1·0% DN
10°

(Lifted 1964)
1912 Namasagali
Bukonte 1928
1926 Kitale

Butere Branch
50 LB
2·0% UP
2·0% DN
17°

Solai Branch
50 LB
1·5% UP
1·5% DN
10°

Thomson's Falls
Branch
50 LB
1·6% UP
1·6% DN
16°

Mbulamuti 1961
Mityana 1953   1931   Tororo   1925
Kasese 1956   Jinja
Kampala
Port Bell 1915
Butere
1932
Kisumu
1901
1901
Mile 543
Turbo
Broderick
Falls 1927
1926
Solai
Thomson's
Falls
1929
Nanyuki 1930
Mt.
Kenya
Naro
Moro
1927

Ruwenzori ▲

Western Uganda
Extension
50 LB
1·5% UP
1·18% DN
10°

Main Line
Jinja-Kampala
80 LB
2·0% UP
2·0% DN
10°

Kisumu Branch
60 LB
2·2% UP
2·2% DN
10°

Nakuru
1900

Main Line Nairobi-Jinja
80/75 LB
1·5% UP
1·5% DN
10°

1899
Mile 362   Thika 1913
Nairobi

Nanyuki Branch
50 LB
3·5% UP
3·0% DN
16°

Magadi
1915

1898
Mile 227

Main Line
Mombasa-Nairobi
95 LB
1·5% UP
1·18% DN
10°

LAMU

...anza 1928

Arusha Branch
45 LB
2·2% UP
2·2% DN
5·8°

Mt. Kilimanjaro ▲   1924   Voi 1897
Arusha   Moshi
1929   1911

Voi-Kahe Branch
50 LB
3·0% UP
3·5% DN
16°

MOMBASA
5/1896

Kinyangiri   1934
Singida
(Lifted 1947)

Tanga Line
60 LB
2·0% UP
2·2% DN
10°

Mombo 1904
1899   TANGA   6/1893
Korogwe
Mruazi Junct.

Kigoma 191...

HISTORY   4.99
SUB-TOTAL   4.99
ITEM CT   1
TOTAL   4.99
CASH TEND   20.00
CHANGE   15.01

EDINBURGH (F5822)
116 NICOLSON STREET
EDINBURGH
EH8 9EJ
www.oxfam.org.uk/shop
11:25 AM (SAT) MATTHEW
01# 1250   21-03-2009

Manyoni
(Lifted 1956)
Hogoro
1947
Kongwa

Mpa...
1949

Central Line
Morogoro-Tabora
56 LB (German)
1·9% UP
1·0% DN
7°

Morogoro
Kilosa
1909
1907

Ruvu Mnyusi Link
55/50 LB
1·5% UP
1·0% DN
10°

1963

Ruvu
Junct.

DAR ES SALAAM
2/1905

Mikumi Branch
50/55 LB
1·5% UP
1·5% DN
10°

Mikumi 1960
Kidatu
1965

Central Line
Dar es Salaam-
Morogoro
60 LB
2·2% UP
2·0% DN
8·7°

Ifakara

1976

Tunduma   Mbeya   Makumbako

Tazara Railway
completed
1976

LINDI
Mkwaya
MTWARA
(Lifted 1963)   1949   Ruo   1954
Nachingwea   Chilungula
Masasi
1958

KEY

95 LB
80 LB
80/75 LB
60 LB
56 LB
55/50 LB
50 LB
50/45 LB
45 LB

Scale in Miles
0   50   100   150

Left: Central Line '26 Class' 'steamer' working boulder-strewn section between Mwanza and Tabora, Tanzania.

Map shows railway lines — main and branch — in East Africa, when built and weight of line laid down.

18

A century ago most of Africa's vast interior lacked any roads, railways or other contemporary means of communication. The only routes into the interior were along numerous rivers, or tortuous caravan trails which were little more than temporary footpaths hacked through the dense forest and bushland.

Even the longest rivers penetrating far inland were not navigable to ocean-going vessels in the way that the Amazon opened up South America, or the Mississippi provided a way into the American West. The mighty Congo River, for example, was blocked by cataracts about 100 miles (160 kms) from its mouth, but beyond it was navigable for hundreds of miles. Similarly the Nile, although an important waterway through Egypt, was impassable in the Northern Sudan because of a series of rapids, yet beyond Khartoum it was open to steamers all the way to Juba and the fertile country bordering on Uganda (and still is).

Although the explorers and foreign traders had been fully familiar with the immense stretches of Africa's coastline for over 300 years, the interior remained a closed book because of difficult terrain, terrible and usually fatal diseases, not to mention the hostility of the tribes fearful of foreign incursions. Even when hardier adventurers did penetrate inland, many savants in Europe preferred to rely on sketchy information provided by geographers of Ancient Greece and Rome, like Herodotus, rather than accept current and accurate reports brought back by contemporaries from their African travels.

In his book 'The African Adventure', Timothy Severin noted: "The falls and rapids of the Congo were so daunting that 300 years after the discovery of its enormous mouth at the end of the 15th Century, white men had charted no more than 130 miles (210 kms) of its lower course. Not until the American, H.M.Stanley, made a small army of porters carry a 45-foot (13.7 m) barge, the 'Lady Alice', in five sections overland did a European boat float on the Congo's broad middle reaches."

Time and again explorers came to grief among the whirlpools and treacherous rapids of Africa's rivers. One of the greatest travellers, Mungo Park, was swept to his death over a waterfall on the River Niger when he had to choose between murderous tribesmen and the turbulent river.

By using shallow draft vessels 19th Century explorers from Europe managed to open up trade routes along West African rivers and David Livingstone adopted a similar method to sail up the Zambezi and its tributary, the Shire River. More determined explorers resorted to carrying sections of boats inland for assembling where rivers were more navigable, or where lakes offered convenient passages.

In East Africa the German explorer, Baron Carl Claus von der Decken, as early as 1865 sailed far up the Juba River in a paddle steamer, but it was wrecked as he was trying to negotiate some rapids and he was speared to death while trying to walk back to the coast.

Preceding pages: Diesel-hauled "down" express passing through the palm belt inland from Mombasa, following virtually the same alignment as the original 1896 track.

Left: Porters carrying steel sections of one of the first steamers to be assembled on shores of Lake Victoria long before the railway line arrived.

Right: Railway surveyor travelling in comfort through rugged upcountry terrain — though most made their own way on foot.

Above: An early survey party in dugout canoes. Where rivers ran, water-borne transport provided easier travel than through dense forest or over rugged mountain terrain.

Right: Horses, mules and oxen were all employed to haul advance parties and materials in building the railways of East Africa — but in many places sleeping sickness in tsetse-fly areas ruled out such transport.

Even so, many people in Europe became obsessed by the possibility they thought African rivers offered for opening up the continent for trade. By the 1880s fanciful plans were being mooted to construct a vast inland north-south waterway in Africa's interior by linking a whole chain of Rift Valley lakes. This route, they visualised, would go all the way from the mouth of the Zambezi through Lake Nyasa and then northwards through Lakes Tanganyika, Kivu and Edward to Lake Albert in north-west Uganda, from which the White Nile flows out into the Sudan and eventually reaches the Mediterranean near Alexandria in Egypt.

This illusion was firmly dispelled by the Scots explorer, Joseph Thomson, during his first expedition to investigate the feasibility of a river or canal link spanning the 200-mile (320 kms) gap between Lake Nyasa and Lake Tanganyika. He found it impossible, not only because of great

Above: Steam traction engines were imported to move very heavy loads for short distances, but in wet weather they quickly became bogged down.

Above: 'Up' goods train nearing Emali — one of the few long straight sections on the Mombasa-Nairobi line.

disparities in the levels of these Rift Valley lakes, but also because of the mountains which blocked the route for such an inland waterway.

One hundred years ago the eastern side of Africa proved far more impenetrable than the rest of the continent because most rivers flowing into the Indian Ocean tumble down from the high inland plateaux with great force, making navigation out of the question. Even the Tana River, which is the largest in what is now Kenya, has such a complicated and constantly-shifting estuary that only very shallow-draught vessels can enter from the sea after negotiating the sandbanks.

The peoples inhabiting the East African hinterland at that time were reputed to be so fierce and warlike that few foreign traders who had settled along the coast felt disposed to risk life and limb by venturing beyond the "palm belt" which then denoted the limit of safety. Those traders safely

*Above: M.V. 'Victoria' offloading cargo at Mwanza,
Lake Victoria, with a '26 Class' steam loco of the
Central Line in foreground. This northern spur of the
main Tanganyika system did not reach Mwanza until
1928 because of the 1914-18 war.*

ensconced on islands like Zanzibar, Pemba and Lamu felt even more secure with a short stretch of water between them and the mainland.

In those days what little trade existed was conducted through African "middlemen", who brought goods to the coastal settlements for barter. Their wares consisted mostly of ivory, rhino horn, skins of all types, and, of course, slaves. By the early 19th Century some of the more intrepid Arab and Swahili traders on the coast began venturing into the interior by forging their own caravan routes and setting up fortified "stations" as far as the Great Lakes (Victoria, Tanganyika and Nyasa).

In their search for goods they could sell profitably at the coast, some of them purchased copper from Katanga and, according to some stories, even gold from the legendary mines of Monomotapa beyond Lake Nyasa. Vast quantities of ivory were also carried to the Indian Ocean from the other lakes, mainly on the backs of slaves captured or bought from compliant chiefs along the route.

At that time the chief caravan routes ran inland through what is now mainland Tanzania from the ports of Kilwa and Bagamoyo, and sometimes from Pangani to the north. From Kilwa the main route lay westwards to the northern limit of Lake Nyasa. But the most important trade route was that starting from Bagamoyo, on the mainland opposite Zanzibar Island. It led westwards as far as present-day Tabora, after which one leg went straight on to Lake Tanganyika at Ujiji, famous as the place where Stanley found Livingstone. The other leg went northwards from Tabora through Karagwe on the west shore of Lake Victoria, eventually reaching the Kingdom of Buganda. This, in turn, linked up with the long and hazardous route through Bunyoro Kingdom and all the way up the Nile valley through the Sudan and Egypt.

Less used was the caravan route that went inland from the coast at Mombasa, skirting what is now Maasailand, then across the trough of the Rift Valley and into the most densely-populated country around the shores of Lake Victoria, leading eventually to Buganda. The main advantage of this was that in spite of the possible dangers in Maasai country it provided the shortest and most direct route from the Indian Ocean to Lake Victoria – in fact it almost halved the time needed to reach the lake.

This route was used mainly for bringing ivory and skins to the coast, but slaves were also brought out. It had long acquired a notorious reputation because of the warlike nature of marauding Maasai warriors and caravans often took wide detours, either south through Chaggaland on the slopes of Mount Kilimanjaro, or through the country of the Wakamba to the north.

So many blood-thirsty tales about this route through Maasailand reached Europe that prospective travellers were effectively dissuaded from using it. When he set out on his first journey across Africa, Henry Morton Stanley chose Bagamoyo as his starting point and deliberately avoided the Maasai country. Claiming that they "delighted in blood", Stanley used to compare them with the Comanche or Apache Indians when addressing audiences in the United States.

It later emerged that many of the reports reaching the outside world were part of a clever "disinformation campaign" carried out by Arab and Swahili traders who were anxious to prevent competition, or any other European interference, in their lucrative – and often illegal – operations. Although grossly exaggerated, the reports had some justification for in 1877 a German botanist, Johannes Hilderbrand, was turned back by Maasai warriors who blocked his way as he tried to pass through their territory.

One man who did not take the stories too seriously was Joseph Thomson, who was chosen by the Royal Geographical Society of Britain to lead its expedition by the direct route to Buganda, as there was a need for speedier communication with the British missionaries already stationed there. Thomson reckoned that by combining guile and bluff with an air of meekness and humility in front of the Maasai, he would avoid any serious confrontation. Violence must be avoided at all costs, he always insisted, and the young Scot put his faith in competent interpreters, so as to avoid any verbal misunderstandings when he encountered warriors looking for trouble, or "sport".

In a journey that took him 14 months, Thomson marched right through Maasailand in 1883 and after a detour to Lake Baringo, he eventually reached the shores of Lake Victoria, and then returned by almost the same route to his starting place on the coast.

Soon merchants in Britain, France and Germany were busy making plans to establish a direct trade route with the King, or Kabaka, of Buganda and neighbouring chiefs, where they were confident a booming market could be created for clothing and other merchandise from Europe.

It was not long before the idea of a railway from the coast to the Lake took shape, for in the same year that Thomson returned to Britain, the powers in Europe were preparing for the historic Berlin Conference which would lay down the broader aspects of the "ground rules" for the ensuing colonial "scramble for Africa".

By 1885 the Treaty of Berlin was signed and spheres of influence allocated to European powers in West Africa and other parts of the continent, notably to Britain and Germany, who had been competing strongly against each other for "rights" over territory in the hinterland of Eastern Africa.

Above: Early Uganda Railway house, on the 'Hill'
Nairobi, still in occupation.

Right: Houses of the same era — 1899 — before the
city developed. The house directly above the 'N Class'
loco — one of the first engines to reach Nairobi — is
believed to have been that of the first Chief Engineer
and General Manager, Sir George Whitehouse.

The railway proposal was just the kind of venture that many politicians in Britain were looking for. After the Treaty of Berlin was signed, the long-standing and bitter rivalry between Britain and Germany in East Africa subsided somewhat and in the more amicable climate the Government in London began to make plans for developing its allotted sphere which was eventually to become Kenya. In Berlin, meanwhile, where the power of Chancellor von Bismarck was waning, the Government began concentrating on developing the territory which later became Tanganyika, or German East Africa.

It was not enough simply to run up a flag and claim that a certain stretch of territory was under the "protection" of the country denoted by the flag. The Berlin Treaty and subsequent conferences made it clear that there had to be tangible signs of development by the colonial power concerned before its claims could be regarded seriously by the other powers. Caravan trails and other rough, impermanent roads through the bush or scrub had little significance since they were either washed away by the seasonal downpours of rain, or were soon obscured by the prolific vegetation and the tropical undergrowth. As a result, those European powers seeking to establish their claims in Africa saw that railways would be one of the best means of showing the sincerity of their intentions.

Things began to move fast once the Treaty of Berlin had been signed and borders drawn on the maps. However, in East Africa there still remained some confusion over the exact extent of the domains belonging to the Sultan of Zanzibar on the African mainland. Successive British Governments had tried to use the Sultan as their instrument of indirect rule in this corner of Africa, whereas the German Governments had favoured a more direct approach, carried to the extreme by their zealous agent, Dr Carl Peters. A Delimitation Conference was therefore convened in 1886 for the express purpose of defining the precise boundaries of the Zanzibari land and during these discussons the question of the "hinterland" which lay beyond the coastline assumed major significance, especially in German eyes.

The principle argued was that whichever European colonial power had sovereignty, or claimed "protection" over, a certain stretch of coastline in Africa, its rights extended inland for an indefinite distance.

This doctrine was largely responsible for the odd pattern of states on the present-day maps of Africa, with narrow strips of land running inland from the coast. It was also to apply to the future states of Kenya and Tanganyika, especially after the Sultan of Zanzibar's claims to mainland East Africa had been bought out by the British and the Germans.

The 1886 Delimitation Conference resulted in an agreement between Britain and Germany on various "terms of reference" for the coming "scramble for Africa", especially on the control of the hinterland, which included the construction of railways among other developments. Significantly, Britain's representative at this conference was Captain Herbert (later Lord) Kitchener, who visited Mombasa and recommended the port as the most suitable starting point for a railway to the interior.

While only a few years before the British Government had been strongly against any official involvement in colonising East Africa, this view changed drastically in the 1880s. Though still reluctant to administer an actual colony, the Conservative Government in London agreed in 1888 that private enterprise should be encouraged to take the initiative in developing the huge stretch of territory inland from Mombasa. As a result, the Imperial British East Africa Company (IBEA) was created by Sir William Mackinnon, a Scots shipping magnate who wanted to develop trade ties with the Kingdom of Buganda. He saw a railway as the only means of opening up a practical trade route through the 700 mile (1,126 kms) undeveloped area between the coast and Buganda, and soon sent out a survey team to plan the route for the railway.

This intervening territory, which Joseph Thomson had already penetrated, was regarded merely as a "corridor" by Europeans who at the time showed little interest in that part of East Africa, but were more concerned with what they saw as the rich and fertile land along the shores of Lake Victoria.

Travellers such as Burton, Speke and Stanley had already brought back glowing accounts of the potential wealth of Buganda and the well-populated land around the lake shore. They also spoke highly of the orderly system of government they found at the court of the local king, or Kabaka, Mutesa. In 1884 Mutesa died and was succeeded by his son, Mwanga. Local observers seemed quite confident that, as his iron-fisted father had done, Mwanga would continue to maintain the peace in Buganda.

Over-optimistic reports about this African kingdom whetted appetites for a speedy trade link with Europe. But then disturbing reports of cruelty and oppression suffered by the subjects of the Kabaka began to come in. These only heightened the desire of Protestant and other missionaries in England to get out to Uganda and minister to those they saw as being in dire need of salvation and the word of God.

The dominant concern of the British Government at the time was geographical – the fact that Buganda occupied a vital strategic position

controlling the source of the White Nile as it poured out of the 26,560 square miles (68,800 square kms) of Lake Victoria to begin a 4,160 mile (6,695 kms) journey to the Mediterranean.

Britain then desperately wanted to gain access to the headwaters of the Nile, as it saw its great potential importance to the Near East, and especially to Egypt where Britain already had a major political and military stake, and also depended upon Egyptian cotton to fuel the ongoing Industrial Revolution. The Suez Canal, recently built by the French engineer, Ferdinand de Lesseps, afforded a quick and easy route to India and the Far East for British ships, instead of the long and hazardous passage round the stormy Cape of Good Hope.

Above: Traditional Maasai 'moran' (warriors) with station master at Singiraini on the Magadi branch line. The station was built during the First World War.

*Above: Wild game still roam the broad Athi Plains,
east of Nairobi. Even a double-headed diesel train fails
to disturb the herds of grazing wildebeest and
hartebeest.*

This rapidly-changing strategic scene pre-occupied most other European nations as well, and France expected that by building the new canal its power and prestige in the Near East would be greatly enhanced. French politicians also saw Egypt as the main centre of influence in the region.

In Germany, Bismarck had never been entirely satisfied with the "carve-up" of East Africa under the terms of the Treaty of Berlin and secretly was highly-covetous of Britain's great influence in Buganda. Ever on the look-out for new avenues to exploit, his agent, Carl Peters, saw the possibility of "leap-frogging" over the British sphere of influence by a cunning stratagem using the tiny enclave of Witu, to the north of Mombasa.

The Sultan of Witu, Ahmed Simba, had fallen out with his Arab neighbours as well as with the British administration, so he was only too happy to sign a treaty in 1885 granting German protection over his so-called "Witu Sultanate", or Swahililand. The German Consul in Witu at the time gained the support of the Berlin Government for a daring plan to lay claim to all the land inland from Witu stretching as far as Buganda, 700 miles (1,126 kms) to the west. Using the powers of the treaty with Witu, Peters sailed up the Tana River secretly and eventually got to Buganda by way of Lake Baringo and across the Rift Valley. At the court of Kabaka Mwanga in Kampala, he signed yet another treaty making that kingdom a German protectorate.

This was the final act in an attempt to encircle Britain's sphere of influence in East Africa in the hope of driving it out altogether and giving Germany undisputed claims to most of East Africa.

Although Carl Peters returned to Tanganyika with a sense of triumph after this long expedition, he was shocked to learn on arrival at the coast that during his long absence in the interior, his government in Berlin had called a temporary truce with Britain and they were no longer rivals in East Africa. As a result of this accommodation, the treaties which Peters had concluded with the Sultan of Witu and the Kabaka in Buganda were considered null and void!

It was at this juncture, when he first learned of the new pact with the British and the agreement to cede influence over Buganda and Zanzibar in exchange for the North Sea Island of Heligoland, that the embittered Peters made the oft-quoted remark deriding the exchange as "two kingdoms in Africa bartered for a bathtub in the North Sea".

This marked improvement in Anglo-German relations took place on the eve of yet another international meeting to discuss developments in East Africa. This time the venue was Brussels, where King Leopold II of

Belgium had been prevailed upon by the British Prime Minister, Lord Salisbury, to call a conference of interested European powers to devise measures "for the gradual suppression of the slave trade on the continent of Africa, and the immediate closing of all external markets which it still supplies".

After deliberating for seven months, the Brussels meeting finally agreed on a Convention aimed at closing all the slave markets in Africa and making slave dealing illegal. In addition to the 13 European countries at the meeting, the United States, the Congo Free State, Persia and Zanzibar were also represented.

Together with Britain and Germany, the other European nations with interests in what the Convention called "the African territories placed under the sovereignty or protectorate of civilised nations" were Belgium, France, Portugal, Spain and Italy.

The Brussels Convention of 1892 spelled out in detail the most effective means the European powers could use to counteract the slave trade in Africa, and Item 3 of the General Act of Brussels clearly recommended: "The construction of roads, and in particular, of railways connecting the advanced stations with the coast, and permitting easy access to the inland waters and to such of the upper courses of rivers and streams as are broken by rapids and cataracts, in view of substituting economical and rapid means of transport for the present means of carriage by men" (porters).

Under the terms of the new treaty the European states, including Britain and Germany, were also given responsibility for opening up their respective concessions by means of "chartered companies". This arrangement was very much to the liking of the British Government which was still most reluctant to become directly involved in colonial adventures in East Africa, already having vast stretches of foreign land under its Imperial yoke. At this stage in British politics there was a certain disillusionment over Imperial "possessions" and when the Liberal Government was in power it was actively promoting its "little England" policy of avoiding further colonial entanglements. Through its chartered company, the IBEA, and treaties made with local rulers such as the Sultan of Zanzibar, Britain had been able to establish its influence over most of the 750,000 square miles (1.9 million square kms) of territory covering what is now Kenya and Uganda. When it suited the Government it usually deferred to Sultan Barghash in Zanzibar as the *de jure* ruler of the hinterland. Germany preferred the more direct approach, and had apparently agreed only reluctantly to the terms of the Brussels Convention.

Although the suppression of slavery was ostensibly a worthy motive which gained considerable domestic support for Governments in Europe, the over-riding reasons for Britain's anxiety to gain physical control over the Kingdom of Buganda was still its strategic importance at the source of the White Nile. This was an even more vital consideration with the Conservative Party in Britain than with the Liberal and other opposition parties, but was nevertheless one of the major pre-occupations of all British statesmen at that time.

Above: Youngsters at play on a little-used rail siding.

Sir William Mackinnon, the shipowner in charge of the IBEA, lost no time in writing to Lord Salisbury, six months after the signing of the Brussels Treaty, suggesting Government assistance for the construction of a 60-mile (96.5 kms) railway inland from Mombasa. He also sought aid for opening up roads and forming "stations" along the route to Lake Victoria.

As a result of this successful appeal, the Director of the IBEA in London was able to send out sufficient materials and rolling stock for building a narrow gauge light railway to cost £50,000. The following year construction got under way, starting from a point on the mainland opposite Mombasa Island, at the head of what has now become Kilindini Harbour.

It was given the very ambitious title of the "Central Africa Railway", and as a symbol of the good intentions of the IBEA to open up the hinterland, sounded very impressive. However the venture got no further than seven miles (11.2 kms) before work stopped. Although it covered no more than a tiny fraction of the distance to Lake Victoria and the source of the Nile, the "Central Africa Railway" did secure a place for itself in history as the first railway to be built in East Africa, albeit no wider than two feet (61 cms) gauge. The tracks were later pulled up and, together with some of the unused rails, were relaid to form a trolley line on Mombasa Island, running from the Old Port, where the Arab dhows anchored, to various Government buildings and Kilindini Harbour. Until 1923 this line was mainly used by Government officials, the more senior of whom had their own trolleys and received monthly allowances to pay the Africans employed to push them.

In its original form the "Central Africa Railway" was used only once for official purposes. It was used, however, as a stylish conveyance for picnic parties venturing inland from the port.

By 1893, the IBEA had withdrawn from Buganda, but remained temporarily at Mombasa until the British Government finally "took the plunge" by declaring a protectorate over the Buganda Kingdom and neighbouring lands as an alternative to outright annexation. It then began to plan for a "proper" railway that would run all the way from the Indian Ocean to Lake Victoria. Not only would this be a really serious indication of Britain's intentions to open up the interior for trade, and combat slavery, but it would be useful for transporting British troops, whom the Government in London thought would be necessary for maintaining a permanent garrison at the source of the White Nile, near Jinja.

For political reasons this latter purpose was deliberately kept quiet in Europe, while full play was given to the anti slavery aspect of the railway so as to disarm those opponents of the Government who were growing restive about the amount of money that would have to be spent on such a remote and risky railway.

Before pulling out of Buganda, the IBEA showed some foresight in commissioning a railway survey to find a route for the proposed line to Lake Victoria. The man chosen for the task was a British Army engineer, Captain J.R.L. MacDonald who arrived in Mombasa to begin work at the end of 1891, ironically just at the time work on the "Central Africa Railway" was abandoned.

Several routes for the railway had already been considered over the extremely rugged landscape between the coast and the lake. The one favoured by Captain F.D. Lugard – a British officer who, as Lord Lugard, was destined to become a heroic figure in Britain's colonial history – would have ascended into the highlands from the small port of Malindi by way of the Sabaki/Athi River valley. This was later rejected in favour of MacDonald's more direct route inland from Mombasa, although it ran into a serious obstacle not far from the coast in the shape of the waterless Taru Desert. This had long posed a serious problem for caravans, whose porters feared the long haul with no water at most times of the year.

MacDonald recommended positioning water tank wagons along the route during construction, with arrangements to have them constantly refilled from Mombasa. Some wagons still in use on the present-day railway bear the instruction: "Not for use beyond Taru" – a reminder of the early days.

In his survey MacDonald constantly had to bear in mind the fact that no earth-moving machinery of any kind existed in the country, nor any material for building bridges or viaducts. These facts ruled out any deep rock cuttings, or high embankments. Nor were any tunnels envisaged in his proposed alignment, even though the railway had to go from sea level to a height of 9,310 feet (2,839 m), and then down to 3,718 feet (1,134 m).

Financed by a £20,000 loan from the British Government, MacDonald and his team of 389 men spent more than a year on the survey, eventually reaching Buganda and its capital, Mengo, in June, 1892 after traversing a total of 4,280 miles (6,848 kms) including many detours and alternative alignments, especially through the rugged country on either side of the Rift Valley. Most of the proposed alignment closely followed the old caravan route established by the IBEA agents on their frequent journeys to Buganda and back to the coast.

*Above: Manual signalling equipment at Mwanatibu,
on the main Nairobi-Mombasa line, Tsavo National
Park, has done good service over many years. In 1985
Kenya Railways began a major conversion to
automatic electronic signalling and communications.*

Much time was spent on finding a suitable way up the western wall of the Rift Valley beyond Nakuru, and MacDonald's final choice passed close to Lugard's military fort and administrative station at Eldama Ravine, then ran up to 3,000 feet (914 m) on the Uasin Gishu Plateau. The descent to Lake Victoria from the highlands would have been along the Nzoia River to an inland lake terminus at Port Victoria in Berkeley Bay, to the west of the Kavirondo Gulf. From there the final 100 miles (160 kms) were to be covered by a 200-ton steamship. MacDonald, who submitted his findings to the British Government on his return to London in 1893, recommended a route which was 657 miles (1,057 kms) long, estimated to cost £2.25 million.

Meanwhile, although the rivalry between the British and the Germans for physical possession of the Buganda Kingdom had subsided temporarily, at this point, Britain saw a grave new threat to its undisputed possession of the Nile Valley developing from another quarter.

By now France was busily extending her influence in Egypt, and displaying her growing interest in the valley of the Nile, on which Egypt was totally dependent for water – and still is to this day. French agents were also active in Ethiopia around the source of the Blue Nile, courting the Amharic ruler, Emperor Menelik II. France had already gained a foothold in the tiny Red Sea enclave of Djibouti, which in 1896 officially became French Somaliland. This considerably strengthened the French moves to counteract British (and Italian) influence in the neighbouring Somali territories, and a railway started by the French in 1897 was eventually to provide the vital rail link between Ethiopia and the outside world through the port of Djibouti. That line however was not completed until 1915.

Eventually, Britain became more concerned over France's strategic ambitions in Africa, than over the local rivalry between British and French missionaries in Buganda which developed into open confrontation between the Church Missionary Society Protestants from London and the Catholic White Fathers from France. In Buganda, the feuding steadily grew worse and Captain Lugard had to resort to strong-arm methods to crush a mutiny, measures which brought much criticism from London and Paris.

All these events made for uncertainty in Britain about the future security of the railway line just as construction was getting under the way. It had originally been intended to push ahead with the line in 1894, the year after MacDonald presented his preliminary survey for approval. But further delays took place which led to criticism in Parliament and caused many politicians to have second thoughts about the wisdom of building such a railway, especially as cost estimates seemed to be soaring year by year.

At the same time, the Germans had not entirely abandoned hope of acquiring part of Lake Victoria, gaining access to Buganda by water, and their thoughts turned to the possibility of a "rival" railway running to the lake through German territory in East Africa, south of Mount Kilimanjaro.

As early as 1891, a company called "Usambara Eisenbahn" had been formed and plans drawn up for a metre-gauge line to run inland from the small port of Tanga as far as the Usambara Mountains, running parallel to the border between German and British territory. An incentive was the rich farming potential of the Usambara mountain range and also the slopes of Mount Kilimanjaro further inland. The Government in Berlin, therefore, favoured an immediate start on the Usambara Railway, in preference to another plan for a Central Railway to run inland from Dar es Salaam towards the Great Lakes.

Work at Tanga began on 30 May, 1893, and two years later the line had reached Muheza, some 25 miles (40 kms) inland. This section became the first "proper" railway built in East Africa, three years ahead of the British-built track from Mombasa to Lake Victoria.

But then a series of bloody uprisings and revolts in various parts of the country caused serious delays to the Germans' construction timetable. Because of this disruption and the sudden bankruptcy of the Usambara Railway Company, no further progress took place on the Usambara line beyond Muheza until 1899, and the plans for the Central Line remained on the shelf until 1904.

Meanwhile, to the north in British-held territory, the situation in Buganda had calmed down sufficiently by 1894 for final plans to be drawn up for the Uganda Railway, in spite of strong opposition in Parliament in London. The appointed engineer, George Whitehouse, arrived in Mombasa the following year and the Government took a dangerous political gamble by sanctioning work to start, even before Parliament had given the authorisation. The first plates were laid at Mombasa on 30 May 1896, three days before the Railway Bill was finally passed in parliament by 255 votes to 75. This vote came after the then Foreign Minister, Lord George Curzon, falsely claimed that British settlers were already arriving in the East Africa Protectorate and had even started planting coffee.

One radical politician, Henry Labouchere, had frequently scoffed at the idea of building a railway in such a remote wilderness and said that the £3.5 million cited as the total cost would be exceeded by at least another £1.5 million. This consistent critic continued his verbal attacks on the Government for sanctioning the line's construction. His scathing poem about the "Lunatic Line" is still quoted today:

> *'What it will cost no words can express*
> *What is its object no brain can suppose*
> *Where it will start from no-one can guess:*
> *Where it is going to nobody knows.*
>
> *What is the use of it none can conjecture:*
> *What it will carry there's none can define:*
> *And in spite of George Curzon's superior lecture,*
> *It is clearly naught but a lunatic line.'*

But, by that stage, the committments had all been made. A "Uganda Protectorate Treaty" in 1894 amounted to virtual annexation of the territory down to a border at the foot of the eastern wall of the Rift and through what is now Lake Turkana. From there to the coast, the previously ill-defined domain of the interior wilderness was *de facto* British and by the end of 1895 the coastal strip itself had been leased from the Sultan of Zanzibar. Strangely, the rent was paid on behalf of the Crown by the financier, Lord Rothschild.

The time and situation in Britain was finally ripe for this "lunatic line to nowhere". In 1897, it was on its way to the lake, well ahead of any rival colonial enterprise in East Africa.

Much had to be done to the port at Mombasa before any construction could start on the railway, even after the decision to go ahead was finally taken. Mombasa at that time was almost exclusively an old Arab town, but with some more recent Portuguese influence. There were very few facilities to support what proved to be a gigantic engineering project.

The railway's Chief Engineer, George Whitehouse, had plenty of experience in building railways in other parts of the world, including Britain, South Africa, India and Mexico. But he was soon to find that the preliminary survey by Captain MacDonald and his team was quite inadequate.

The survey in 1891 had been hastily carried out on the assumption that a much more detailed investigation of topography, soils and so on, would precede actual construction work.

However, in their desire for speed at all costs, the British Government did not think this was necessary and fully expected Whitehouse to complete the railway through some of the most rugged terrain in Africa on the scantiest of information, while at the same time sticking to the very rough cost estimates. Of course the initial £3.5 million estimates fell far short of the eventual figure, even allowing for the inflation caused by a delayed start.

Even before the tracks could move off Mombasa Island, a great deal of preparatory work was needed. Although Kilindini was ideal as a deep-water anchorage, there were no wharves or unloading installations and the Old Harbour on the opposite side of the island only handled Arab dhows and a few small steamships plying the Indian Ocean routes.

First, a strong jetty had to be built as a temporary arrangement so that some of the heavier equipment could be brought ashore quickly.

In the meantime, unloading of the lighter cargoes took place at a beach near Kilindini Harbour, but only at high tide. This limited the number of hours devoted to unloading, although the time element was critical.

While time was one of the scarcest commodities for the workers on the Uganda line, water on Mombasa Island was even scarcer, once the army of imported labourers from Asia began to arrive. To cope with this rapidly-expanding population, the meagre water supply was augmented by every available means. Whitehouse resorted to building a series of catchments for the rainwater which fortunately fell abundantly at certain times of the year.

To boost this erratic supply, he also dammed a major stream on the mainland nearby. In November 1896, a water distillation plant which could produce 12,000 gallons (54,552 litres) of fresh water a day from the salt water arrived from Europe. This was needed not only for the island population and the railway workers, but also to supply the "water trains" operating 100 miles (160 kms) up the line to – and beyond – the waterless Taru Desert.

One of the problems in procuring urgent material from Britain at that time was the lack of any direct shipping service between London and Mombasa. All such cargoes had to be transhipped at Aden, as no British India Steam Navigation Company (BISN) vessel had served Mombasa since the company withdrew from Uganda. The only direct communications were with India, and consisted of four ships a month – two German and two British – which called at Mombasa on the way to

Preceding pages: Passenger train enters the Mazeras 'snake' — one of several spiral sections devised by the engineers laying the original Uganda Railway in order to gain altitude rapidly on the steep ascent from the coastal plateau to the inland plateaux. This spiral still follows its original 1896 alignment.

Top left: Railway materials were offloaded from lighters at Kilindini Beach, Mombasa, until a pier was completed.

Top Right: As no earth-moving equipment was then available, the major earthworks on the Uganda Railway were built solely by gangs of labourers brought from India.

Above left: Skilled Indian stone-masons cutting rock near the Tsavo railhead with surveyor, shaded by umbrella, taking measurements.

Above right: Virtually the whole of the Uganda Railway was laid on steel sleepers to prevent ravages of termites. Stone ballast to stabilise the track was often in short supply locally.

Right: Stern-faced Robert O. Preston (front left on inspection trolley) supervised the entire plate-laying operation over the 580 mile (930 kms) stretch from Mombasa to Lake Victoria. He was accompanied all the way by his wife, Florence.

Top left: Tracklaying gangs were ferried daily from their camps to railhead usually 10 to 16 miles (16 to 25 kms) ahead.

Top right: One of the Baldwin 'B Class' locomotives imported from the U.S.A. because of strikes in British engineering works.

Above: Viaduct at Mazeras was built from imported timber. At this stage the rich upcountry forests were too remote to be exploited.

Right: The first passenger train to leave Mombasa in January 1898, hauled by 'UR 35' an early British-built engine of a type also then in use in India. Some of these 'F Class' locos remained in service until the 1930s.

Zanzibar, then the main seaport on the East African coast.

A vanguard group of 350 Indian labourers had arrived in Mombasa just one month after Whitehouse. By 1896 there were 2,000 of them, including many skilled craftsmen – carpenters, stonemasons, smiths, clerks, surveyors and draughtsmen. By the time the Uganda railway reached its inland terminus on Lake Victoria some 33,000 labourers had been brought from India, many returning to make way for others.

As the labour force swelled, frantic efforts were made to build accommodation for them on Mombasa Island. Houses for senior officials had been very simply constructed – usually galvanised iron shacks, shielded from the hot sun by *makuti* (thatch) roofing made from palm fronds taken from the hundreds of coconut trees which had been felled to make way for the rail yards and storage dumps. For the Indians, even simpler buildings were put up, consisting of plain mud walls, palm tree trunks for supports and *makuti* roofing. Improvements had to wait until later.

Much has been written about the decision to use Indian labour on the Uganda Railway instead of local African workers – and various reasons have been given. The most likely explanation is that in those days this part of East Africa was still seen (in Britain at least) as an appendage of India. British officials, especially the military men, were mostly seconded from service in India, but their experience there was very different from what they were to encounter in Africa. Indian labourers already had considerable experience of building railways in India itself, and the narrow gauge-lines built there were all of metre gauge, the same as that used on the Uganda Railway. While local Africans were recruited as porters, their unfamiliarity with the tools needed for track-laying and railway maintenance meant that they would have to spend valuable time being instructed in the rudiments of engineering, and as the pressure from London continued time was still valuable.

Another important disadvantage in using local people for railway work in general began to emerge once the line progressed inland. Most tribespeople, especially men, were reluctant to serve far from their home villages and families, and those who did agree to work away from home proved unreliable. In many cases, they simply deserted after a time, while others proved highly susceptible to climatic changes of even a few degrees, so that a much higher percentage were on the sick list as compared to the hardier Indian workers, who worked consistently well for the equivalent of only five dollars a month. But when the line reached terrain with drastic changes in altitude and temperatures, it was found wiser to choose Tamils and others from South India on the hot, humid lowlands, and Pathans and other hill people in the cooler areas above 5,000 feet (1524 m).

*Above: Early morning outside Mombasa Station after
the arrival of the overnight train from Nairobi.*

In Mombasa work had to start early on workshops and storage facilities
as a back-up to the railway construction. These buildings had to be fairly
solid to give adequate protection against the damp and humidity of the
rainy seasons, as well as against theft.

The amount of material ordered for the railway was impressive. For the
tracks to reach Lake Victoria, a route of over 600 miles (965 kms), it had
been calculated that it would be necessary to order 200,000 lengths of
30-foot (10.2 m) rail, each weighing 500lbs (226 kgm) with another 200,000
fishplates and 400,000 bolts to secure the rails to 1.2 million sleepers.

Most of the sleepers were to be made of steel, because wood was
considered too vulnerable to attack from termites and the usual creosote
preservative tended to be washed off by the heavy rain. Nearly five million
steel keys were needed to keep the rails in place and many heavy steel
girders of varying sizes were required for the numerous culverts, bridges

and viaducts. Once individual designs had been completed, these all had to be specially measured and transported. The island soon became a hive of activity, in contrast to its former sleepy character. Even the pristine beaches of white sand became temporary dumps for construction material. Oil slicks stained the blue waters of the Kilindini Creek. It took four months for Whitehouse and his men to provide a suitable base and infrastructure for the line to move out of the port-town.

Finally, the great day dawned when the first locomotives arrived by ship from India, even though they were 20-year-old workhorses, almost at the end of their useful lives – two second-hand "A" Class engines from the Indian State Railways' metre gauge system. Fortunately all they were needed for at that time was to haul newly-arrived material from the beach to the railway stacking yards on the island.

The only other transport on the island at that time was the "Mombasa Trolley", consisting of seven miles (11 kms) of narrow 2-ft (0.6m) gauge track which had been built through the narrow streets of the port to connect the Old Harbour with a number of Government offices, including the Customs House. These trolley lines had been part of the "Central Africa Line" tracks and they were relaid in Mombasa for the benefit of senior officials with their own push-trolleys.

Everything was now ready for the first rails to be laid down at the Mombasa terminus. The historic ceremony took place on 30 May, 1896, and was recorded for posterity by contemporary photographers – a truly Victorian scene that could have been at a Royal garden party in London. There were moustachioed officials with straw "boaters" and military types in dress uniforms and solar pith helmets.

Their ladies sat demurely in long, voluminous dresses and "cartwheel" hats. On one side, standing obediently to attention, was a group of Indian sepoys forming the guard of honour for the auspicious occasion.

Despite all this pomp and circumstance, the line did not progress more than a couple of miles (three kms or so) before encountering the first of many obstacles – getting off Mombasa Island and on to the vast and largely uncharted African mainland. Barring the way were the shallow waters of Makupa Creek with its mangrove-covered mudbanks. As the tidal creek was quite narrow, MacDonald thought a simple earth embankment or causeway would do the job, but he had overlooked the fact that small dhows and canoes had to pass along the channel.

The metal parts for a permanent bridge, later to be renamed the Salisbury Bridge before its present-day name of Makupa Causeway was substituted, were still being fabricated in a far-off British yard and were not due for some months. Desperate, Whitehouse decided on a temporary wooden structure to bridge the creek. But while there were trees in the vicinity, no-one knew anything about their suitability for bridge-building. Extensive forests containing good hardwoods were known to exist in the uplands of the hinterland, but there were no means of transporting such heavy logs – until the railway had been completed.

When it was discovered that the waters in Makupa Creek were infested with various insects, such as borer beetles which could eat their way into wooden bridge supports, Whitehouse was finally convinced that he should use only timbers imported from Europe.

And so this major work was delayed for a further eight months until the special consignment of timber arrived. In the meantime, work-gangs set about levelling the route on the mainland in preparation for laying the rails ahead of the bridge opening. This took place with due ceremony in August, 1896.

A rise in elevation of 500 feet (152 m) over the next 15 miles (24 kms) inland posed a further engineering problem which the construction men overcame by building a "spiral" section of track which doubled back on itself by means of a bridge. Considerable earthworks also had to be built on this section, and as only picks and shovels were available for these embankments and cuttings, progress was slow. Since then the alignment up this steep rise has been repeatedly improved, the last re-alignment being completed as recently as 1983.

Above: First-class coach now at Nairobi Railway Museum in original livery of the old Uganda Railway.

Right: Sole survivor of 27 wood, coal or oil burning shunting tank engines acquired by the Kenya Uganda Railway, in its original livery at Nairobi Railway Museum.

Right: Articulated Garratt locomotive from Beyer-Peacock of Manchester, UK, went into service in 1940 as 'Karamoja'. Now in 'retirement' at Nairobi Railway Museum with the original Kenya Uganda Railway (KUR) livery.

In response to London's demand for a speed-up in the construction schedule, Whitehouse sent three survey teams ahead of the construction gangs working at the railhead. One travelled as far as the Kikuyu Escarpment just beyond where Nairobi stands today, and checked out the approach to the steep eastern wall of the Rift Valley – the most serious physical obstacle on the entire route. A second survey party went to Kibwezi some 200 miles (320 kms) up the line and worked its way back towards Mombasa eventually to link up with the third team moving inland along the railhead from the coast. For this latter team, the terrain was to prove extremely hard going.

In the immediate hinterland, undergrowth and creepers became so dense and thorny that by the time the railhead reached a wide ravine at Mazeras, the construction gangs were already right on the heels of the survey party who were moving at the rate of only 300 yards (275 metres) a day.

Above: Late afternoon light catches the upcountry passenger train as it negotiates the Mazeras spiral a few miles out of Mombasa.

Right: Still in use today, manual signal levers from the 'Railway Signal Co. Limited' of Liverpool bear the initials 'UR' — Uganda Railway.

Right: Ingenious form of inspection trolley — an improvised bicycle — was used for many years to inspect the permanent way. It is preserved in Nairobi Railway Museum.

It was more than just thick bush, however, which held things up at this stage. In 1896 the coast became inflamed with revolt when the Mazrui Arabs rose against the British Administration and the Sultan of Zanzibar. The uprising, although it only affected parts of the coast, put an end to most field work for a time until imported Indian troops suppressed the revolt and chased the rebel leaders into German East Africa.

Opposite: Only two of these 2-6-2 wheel arrangement shunting tank locos were in service — at terminals — from 1950 until the end of the steam era in East Africa at the end of the 1970s.

Spanning the Mazeras Ravine with a wooden viaduct took yet another month and then torrential rains halted work for three weeks. At that point, a full year after work had started, the Uganda Railway had progressed only 23 miles (36 kms) from Mombasa. Prospects for further advance were not encouraging, since workers were already ill with malaria, tropical ulcers, dysentery and pneumonia. In this kind of country, every minor scratch soon turned into a festering sore, taking a long time to heal. On occasions, because of sickness of one sort or another, fully half the labour force was out of action.

In February, 1897, a new arrival, whose name would become prominently linked with the successful building of the Uganda Railway, appeared on the scene from India. This was Ronald O. Preston, who was placed in charge of the plate-laying gangs slowly moving the railway westward. Like most other senior construction officials, Preston had spent many years working as foreman platelayer on the Indian Railways. With him was his wife, Florence, who was to accompany him along the entire length of the track to the shores of Lake Victoria. Four years later, she would see the embryo port-town named Port Florence in her honour. It was later re-named Kisumu.

Above: One of the largest of all the Garratt articulated locomotives used on the East African Railways system, a '59 Mountain Class' engine, 'Mount Shengana' working oil tankers.

Preston lost no time in getting down to work and speeding up the tempo of the construction gangs. He was soon to experience the rigours of construction work in Africa. When travelling in a railway wagon to the railhead the day after disembarking at Kilindini, he asked for soap to wash off the dirt and grime from the trip. "Yes, we can give you a lump of soap", he was told, "but there is not a drop of water left in the camp, as we put the last into the kettle for tea." The constant shortage of water became even more acute once the Taru Desert was reached, and lasted almost 100 miles (160 kms) until the approach to Voi. Many of the workers used what putrid water they could find and strained it through their dusty turbans, only to find it brackish and most unpalatable. Preston's "remedy" was to mix a spoonful of Eno's fruit salts with the green slime that passed for water. The fizzing action left a frothy, green scum on top and clear water beneath.

The construction rate was speeded up once Preston found that the Indian labourers were being paid a fixed wage, regardless of the amount of work they did. He introduced a form of "piece work" to give them some incentive to work harder. His new system of payment by the mile of track laid made a great difference to the men's spirits, as well as their productivity.

A river containing salty water presented the Chief Engineer, Whitehouse, with his first real challenge. Steel girders were brought up to the railhead on the edge of this river, known locally by its Swahili name *Maji ya Chumvi* (River of Salt). However, there were no means of lifting the heavy girders because mobile steam cranes had not yet been provided for construction work away from Mombasa, nor was there any stone in the vicinity suitable for building supports for the girders.

Whitehouse improvised a system of erecting "sleeper cribs", which were trestle-towers built out of wooden sleepers laid in the middle of the river, with rails led out over the flimsy structure above the 30-foot (9.1 m) gorge. He then moved flatcars carrying 40-foot (12 m) girders, each weighing 20 tons, across the gap. Once these were levered into position with crowbars and heavy wooden sleepers placed at each end for the girders to rest on, the rails could then be pulled out and relaid in their proper position once the bridge was complete.

This lack of stones near the coast created more problems during construction. Not only could the engineers find no stones with which to build culverts and bridges, but there was not even any to make gravel, essential for ballasting the track. Much of the line had to be laid over compacted soil until rock deposits were found further inland and used as stone quarries.

Laying mile upon mile of track became a monotonous and extremely wearying task in the hot, arid landscape. According to one contemporary description:

'The men were out of their tents at sunrise every day, clambering sleepily aboard the materials train that would carry them forward to the head of the tracks. Here, rails and sleepers were quickly taken off the flatcars and stacked on the ground, while the train reversed to camp for its next load. Then the steel pathway began to inch ahead in a sort of limping, leap-frog fashion. One gang placed the sleepers in rough alignment along one or two hundred yards of embankment. On their heels came teams of two men carrying 30-foot rail lengths, slung from poles on their shoulders. 'When the rails had been laid on the sleepers, a third gang joined the individual track sections with rectangular steel fishplates, secured by fish-bolts. Still another crew clipped the rails into the lugs of the sleepers, each rail length being tamped down with the blow of a sledgehammer and fixed even more firmly to the sleepers with steel keys, driven home by keying hammers. When the entire section had been laid down, it was slewed into correct alignment with crowbars. All this took anywhere from between three and six hours. By then the materials train would have returned with at least one more load of tracks and sleepers. The process was repeated all day.'

Day after day, waterless, and scorching under the merciless sun, the gangs toiled on through the wastes of the Taru Desert, cheered by only the sight of the next 'water train' chugging up from the coast to slake their raging thirsts. Sometimes these life-giving trains were held up and there was much suffering until the water eventually reached the railhead workers. In spite of the hard work and the terrible conditions, however, deaths in the first year were remarkably low at only 100 men, so the recovery rate from the various tropical diseases must have been commendable.

Once beyond Voi, in the shadow of the Taita Hills, the going was much easier and local labour was more plentiful for porterage and even for earth-moving. But an acute shortage of wagons caused more delays in bringing up material to the railhead and mechanical trouble with the aged locomotives continued until the end of 1897, when Whitehouse received another long-awaited shipment to augment the decrepit 15 engines which had kept things moving during the previous two years.

Five of the new arrivals were "F" Class locomotives in common use in India, but specially fitted for use on the Uganda Railway, with outsize cow-catchers in front like the "iron horses" of the Wild West. They were also notable for the outsize domes on top of their boilers and huge headlamps in front of the chimneys. The 0-6-0 wheel arrangement, though unbecoming, enabled the engines to travel over the poorly-aligned sections of track with few derailments. Since there were no means of lifting heavy locos other than pulleys and manpower, or oxen if available, derailments were the cause of serious delays. When they did occur, these were usually caused by washaways.

One observer summed up the merits of these new engines in these words: "Despite their diminutive nature, these engines packed all the muscle needed to negotiate the stiff gradients and sharp curves that leaped and twisted along every mile of track to the lake."

But there were only five of them. Another 25 on order lay unfinished still in the maker's yard in Britain, where a strike held up their completion for months. They were badly missed on the construction work between Mombasa and Nairobi. Somehow Whitehouse had to make do with the five new locos and keep the other 10 rickety veterans going as long as possible.

Even when as many as half of these were operational at one time, he had to cope with mass sickness among the engine drivers. At one time, malaria put 11 of the 12 drivers out of action. Everything then depended upon the one lone stalwart driving the engine.

External events also continued to have serious adverse effects on construction work, as if the many local troubles were not enough. By 1898, the South African War between the British and the Boers had broken out and much of Britain's attention was diverted to the southern clash which called for many British troops to be sent there.

Shipping space for the Uganda Railway supplies became hard to obtain and as support for the "war-effort" mounted to fever pitch in Britain, so concern about the men struggling to build a "lunatic line" into the heart of Africa noticeably waned. Meanwhile, Preston and the others suddenly found themselves fighting their own little war along the railway line. This broke out once the railhead had reached the fast-flowing and deep Tsavo River and work came to a halt while preparations were made to build a bridge. In the emptiness of the Taru Desert there had been few animals to shoot for the pot, but when they reached the Tsavo things changed drastically.

The first warning that sinister happenings were about to occur came early in 1898, just after the Tsavo River had been spanned by a temporary wooden bridge. A platelayer suddenly disappeared and was eventually discovered near the river's edge, all the flesh torn from his corpse, but with his head and feet still intact.

This was a sure sign that a lion had been at work, and confirmation came with the evidence of paw marks around the body. Parties were sent out in pursuit of the man-eating lion, not a common occurrence. Several days went by with no sign of any animal. Suddenly one night the workers were awakened with shouts of "Sher!" (tiger!). Preston and his companion hunters leapt out of their tents as the camp reverberated to the sound of drums banging out the alarm. It was then that they learned that a second labourer had been dragged off by the nocturnal marauder.

Naturally panic broke out at the railhead and things became worse when the second corpse was found. Always one to take advantage of adversity, Preston persuaded the frightened Indian workers that the quicker they got the railway line moving and shifted their railhead camp, the safer they would be.

"We were generally fairly quick at shifting camp, but this one move from Tsavo was certainly a record", Preston recalled later in his memoirs.

Although the platelaying gang were lucky to escape without further attacks from the lions at Tsavo, the engineer following them up the line to erect a permanent steel bridge was not so fortunate. As an Indian Army Officer, Colonel J.H.Patterson, had long experience of life in the bush, and bridges such as the one he had to construct at Tsavo held no qualms for him. However, he had not bargained for man-eating lions – not just a lone "rogue" male, but a lion and lioness hunting as a pair.

The result was that the bridge which should have taken him less than four months to complete, took Patterson almost a year.

Patterson recounted in his best-selling book "Man Eaters of Tsavo" how this bridge was one of the largest engineering works after Makupa Causeway outside Mombasa. It required a 300-foot (91 m) span of girders over the river, supported by three strong stone piers.

Despite the constant hum of activity as the bridge-builders slogged away, the man-eating lions were not scared off, but lay low, waiting for their opportunity. Of course, Patterson was well aware of their previous attacks and had his men keep a sharp look out at all times. He had not been entirely convinced that the two previous victims had been killed by lions, inclining to the belief that they had been murdered by their fellow workers. He wrote at the time: "I thought it quite likely that some scoundrel had murdered them for their money".

Patterson's scepticism was eventually dispelled when one of his Sikh employees was snatched from his tent one night and dragged by a lion into the bush. On closer inspection of the gruesome site where the hapless Indian had put up a futile struggle, Patterson came to the conclusion that not one but two lions were involved.

Realising the effect this news would have on the camp's morale, he quickly organised a lion hunt. Little did he know at the time that the hunt would last for ten months, seriously delaying progress on this vital bridge that had to be completed before heavy supply trains could pass up the line with material urgently needed for the difficult sections ahead.

Night after night he was out with his .303 rifle and some Indian marksmen, and while he heard lions roaring and even the sounds of further victims being attacked, Patterson could never get close enough to finish one off. Work continued unhindered in the daytime, but at night when the lions were on the prowl, in spite of huge bonfires and all the tents protected with barricades of sharp thorns, sleep was almost impossible.

Below: Lowering sun falls on the down 'mail' train from Nairobi to Kisumu — its diesel locomotive in the original green and yellow livery of the E.A.R.&H. system — as it descends the Rift Valley escarpment at Kijabe.

The lions' senses seemed almost uncanny, for they always found weak spots in the camp defences to make their strikes. Even the camp hospital became a target and there they wreaked havoc in the tent clinics, mauling those patients too weak to flee for their lives.

The frustrated Patterson, in spite of his tiger-hunting days in India, was beside himself with despair before he finally caught sight of the man-eaters when one tried to spring at him as he was waiting in ambush for the chance to shoot. His shots managed to deflect the beast just as it was about to spring, but he failed to register a hit. "Except as food, they showed complete contempt for human beings", Patterson wrote later, adding, "shots, shouting and firebrands they alike held in derision."

As the hunt continued, news of the man-eaters' presence filtered down to Mombasa and elsewhere and the area around Tsavo was soon being scoured by scores of "hunters", many of them civil servants or military men on leave, while others were international sporstmen who had come from afar to join in the challenge of hunting the "man-eaters". The night air soon echoed to the crack of Winchester rifles, augmented by Sniders and Remingtons. Inevitably there was a near-massacre of the local lion population, but always the man-eaters managed to evade the fusilades.

Among those sportsmen who visited the railhead at Tsavo during this period was Lord Delamere, who was later to play a leading role in developing Kenya as a Colony and especially in the expansion of the railway system throughout East Africa.

The year 1898 was almost over when a mass desertion of Indian labourers took place. A daily supply train was on its way past Tsavo to Mombasa to collect more railway supplies when the driver suddenly spotted a mass of human bodies lying on the rail track ahead. He braked violently and as the train was still skidding to a stop, the bodies rose up and hundreds of panicky workers swarmed on to the wagons. Despite Patterson's attempt to stop the train and call back the deserters, the train picked up speed again and chugged off with its cargo of frightened labourers on board.

Patterson was left with only fifty or so men who loyally remained behind to help finish the job, man-eaters or not. Eventually on 9 December, 1898, Patterson killed the first of the man-eating lions after several near-misses, but it took him a further three weeks before he dropped the second, ending the long reign of terror which made the insignificant river crossing at Tsavo (which in the local vernacular means "slaughter") a notorious name, long to be remembered. The two stuffed animals can be seen today on display in the Marshall Field Museum in Chicago.

But the bloody saga of the 'Man-eaters of Tsavo' was by no means ended with the crossing of the river. At a place called Kima, further up the line, there was a tragic incident a year later when another lion crept stealthily into a railway coach one night. Inside was a Railway Police Inspector, Charles H. Ryall, waiting with his rifle cocked to blast the man-eater. Drowsy during a night-long vigil, he had just begun to doze off when the lion entered the carriage. One blow from its paw broke Ryall's neck and in a single leap the lion carried his corpse out the open window and into the darkness. All along this semi-arid stretch of country between Voi and Machakos lions proved one of the great hazards facing the rail construction teams, although it is rare indeed for lions to seek out human flesh unless too old or too crippled to hunt other animals.

Always there was the insistent pressure from London for faster progress on the construction. Speed had improved markedly since the funereal progress of the very early days when it was moving at a snail's pace. At that tempo, reckoned civil servants in London, it would be 1924 before the railway would reach the shores of Lake Victoria.

By mid-1897, however, things were moving at a fair pace and the arrival of large numbers of animal transport – mostly oxen, donkeys and some horses and even camels – helped to move heavier objects. It was at this time that Preston was alarmed to find that a derailed train down the line was actually carrying a large contingent of troops, just arrived from India. He soon realized that the railway he was helping to build was not only to reach the source of the Nile and open up the fertile lands around it, but was also designed to provide a rapid means of transport for a large military force being assembled by the British in the interior.

In fact, by the end of 1897 no less than 300 tons of military stores and about 2,600 soldiers had been ferried up from Mombasa to the railhead, considerably reducing the time and trouble it would have taken if men and material had travelled all the way on foot.

A state of near-panic had developed back in London when the British Government learned that the French were serious about wanting a hand in controling the Nile Valley. So determined were the French, they had already dispatched a small force of soldiers under Captain Jean-Baptiste Marchand by boat from Brazzaville, on the Atlantic coast, to rendezvous on the banks of the White Nile with another French party coming from Ethiopia.

Marchand's orders were to consolidate his hold on the Nile at a place called Fashoda, north of present-day Malakal, then lay claim to a stretch of the vital waterway in the name of France. But the plan misfired when the party from Ethiopia arrived at Fashoda first, well ahead of Marchand who was paddling painstakingly in his metal craft, little bigger than a bathtub, more than 2,000 miles (3,200 kms) up the Congo River and its tributary, the Oubangui. Marchand, with 11 French officers and 100 Senegalese troops, eventually crossed the watershed into the Nile Valley and floated down the Bahr-el-Ghazal to reach Fashoda – only to discover that his compatriots had been and gone.

It was then 1898 and the British forces, under Major-General Sir Herbert Kitchener, had already defeated the army of the Mahdi at Omdurman, opening the Nile to free navigation after a blockade by the Mahdist forces which lasted 14 years. When he heard of Marchand's arrival, Kitchener promptly sailed up the river from Khartoum to Fashoda, and coldly greeted the 12-man French party and their Senegalese escorts when they boarded the British general's gunboat for a formal reception. Kitchener at once made it clear that there was no question of establishing a French enclave on the River Nile to threaten Britain's monopoly over this vital waterway.

Already shattered by this news, Marchand was even more distressed to receive a signal from Paris ordering an immediate withdrawal from Fashoda. It was an ironic echo of the Carl Peters fiasco earlier, and Marchand returned home by way of Ethiopia, rather than suffer the humiliation of a voyage down the British-controlled Nile. Thus was averted an extremely delicate political situation which could have led to a war in Europe.

By now the British Government had conceded that its main purpose in building the railway to Uganda was to provide Britain with a quick and convenient route to the Nile's headwaters and to the Kingdom of Buganda, so that it could thwart any rival bids by other European powers.

While the "Fashoda Incident" ended further French attempts to interfere with Britain's control of the Nile Valley, pressure continued on speeding up the Uganda Railway's progress, as this remained a top priority in Britain's plans for developing the East African hinterland. By this time the British Prime Minister had been able to claim that the line creeping inland from Mombasa was part of a British "flanking move" from the Indian Ocean which had out-manoeuvred France's "pincer-move" on the Nile.

Like many other developments in Eastern Africa at that time, the Uganda Railway was inspired by events in Europe as much as by happenings in Africa itself. It was a lucky coincidence, however, that the route followed by the railway led through the fertile and well-watered highlands of Kenya, rather than through the deserts of the northern two-thirds of the country. It meant that in the years to come Kenya had a convenient rail route to serve some of the most potentially-productive farmland in all Africa.

But that time was still far off. Once the Athi River had been reached at Mile 309 at the western limits of the Kapiti Plains, the Ngong Hills were already on the horizon and the swampy area on which the future capital would arise, with its impressive skyline of tall, elegant buildings, was only a few miles distant.

Over the plains the speed of construction was roughly half a mile (close to one km) a day, so when the Governor of German East Africa arrived to inspect progress on the Uganda Railway in 1899, the platelayers, through their training, were in a good position to put on a special "rush job" for his benefit. The Germans had only just resumed construction of their line inland from Tanga. As Chief Engineer of the Uganda Railway, Whitehouse thought it appropriate that his visitor be suitably impressed by the work taking place to the north of their common border. With well-greased nuts and bolts, a hand-picked, highly-practised plate-laying gang excelled themselves on the day of the demonstration by laying a fraction over one mile (1.6 kms) of track.

According to Preston, who had supervised the operation, he later received a telegram from Whitehouse telling him that the track-laying exercise had so impressed the German governor that "he had come to the conclusion that it was hopeless for them to hope to get to the lake before us". It might well have been a historic day, for the Germans across the border made no serious attempt to reach Lake Victoria after that and by 1912, the Tanga line had reached no further than Moshi at the foot of Kilimanjaro.

As the track was being laid for the final approach to Nairobi, the Uganda Railway Committee in London decided to send out an expert to check on progress and take a look at the proposed alignment which lay ahead, where many physical obstacles barred the way.

After two months in Kenya, the expert, Sir Guildford Molesworth who had already visited construction during the ill-fated Tsavo period, reported back to London: "Greater progress could not possibly have been expected. In fact, taking into consideration the very great difficulties that have been encountered, the advance of the railhead has been remarkably rapid".

Molesworth also drew London's attention to the benefits which the new railway had already brought to the local scene, and observed: "The porters of all up-country caravans now travel as far as possible by railway, and the terrible march across the Taru Desert has become a thing of the past. The civilising influence of the railway is most marked, even in the uncompromising region which it has hitherto traversed. The tribes in contact with it have already commenced to trade and a demand for European goods is springing up amongst them".

'Nyrobi', as the railwaymen first spelled it, was reached by the rails on 30 May, 1899. Maasai living in the area called the swampy ground on the edge of the Kikuyu forest, *'Nakusentolon'*, meaning 'the beginning of all beauty'. Preston was less impressed. He described the dreary vista as a "bleak, swampy stretch of soggy landscape, devoid of human habitation of any sort, the resort of thousands of wild animals of every species." The actual origin of the word 'Nairobi' comes from the small stream then bisecting the swamp and called by the Maasai 'place of cold water' (*Ulase en-airobe* in their Maa language). Today this stream is known as the Nairobi River, and flows through the centre of Kenya's capital.

Once the railway reached the flat ground around Nairobi, the surrounding area soon filled with railway material of every description. For Whitehouse this was the main reason for choosing the site – the level terrain was ideal for building the railway yards, station facilities and workshops that he realised would be necessary for the formidable challenge that lay ahead, the trough of the Great Rift Valley. Moreover, being 327 miles (523 kms) distant from Mombasa, this was roughly the half-way point to the Lake terminus, which was then still planned for Port Victoria.

The railhead camp quickly mushroomed into a rough-and-ready township that resembled a "cow town" of about the same period in the American West. Lines of tents pitched haphazardly were interspersed with more substantial buildings of corrugated, galvanised iron sheeting. Hardly a single tree stood on the desolate site to provide shade from the Equatorial sun, its rays even stronger because of the rarefied air at the mile-high altitude. When the rains came, the black cotton soil soon became a quagmire which held all wheeled traffic firmly in its grip.

There was then one single street, proudly called Victoria Street after the Mistress of the Empire whose purpose the railway was destined to serve. At one end of the street was the beginning of a "shopping centre", consisting of a cluster of tightly-packed Indian stores. A two-storey wood and iron edifice proudly announced itself as "Wood's Hotel", the only hostelry away from the coast. But it was another of these faceless wood and iron bungalows which became a magnet attracting civil servants and railway officials alike for their social diversions. It was grandly called "The Club".

Some respectability was bestowed on this collection of shacks when the Foreign Office in London directed that the Provincial Headquarters of Ukamba be moved from Machakos to Naïrobi. A few years later, Nairobi was elevated to the glorified status of the Headquarters of the East Africa Protectorate in place of Mombasa, but it was still a far cry from the bustling, thriving metropolis, and commercial centre for East Africa, that it has become today.

As Nairobi took shape, the railway engineers were busy tackling their greatest challenge so far. Ahead lay a 2,000 foot (600 m) climb up the gradient known as the Kikuyu Escarpment. This led past Limuru to the lip of the Rift Valley's steep eastern wall, posing an even greater engineering problem. Whitehouse, now installed in Nairobi, set about laying the rails out of Nairobi and up the old caravan route to Limuru. At the same time, others were at work creating the railway's future "nerve-centre", installing the entire apparatus of the Railway Headquarters which had to be moved up from Mombasa.

Preston was later to recall the magnitude of the tasks which faced him in mid-1899. "There was an immense amount of work to be done in converting an absolutely bare plain, 327 miles distant from the nearest place where even a nail could be purchased, into a busy railway centre. Roads and bridges had to be constructed, houses and workshops built, turntables and station quarters erected, a water-supply laid on and 101 other things which go into the making of a railway township. Wonderfully soon, however, the nucleus of the present town began to take shape."

The Railway Chief's chosen site, dictated by his own immediate needs, was hardly one that town planners would have recommended had they been around at the time. The nature of the swampy terrain provided a breeding ground for malaria-carrying mosquitoes and brought many problems in years to come.

Sir Charles Eliot, the first Commissioner of the East Africa Protectorate, was quite blunt about the site when he was transferred to Nairobi from Mombasa in 1901:

"Nairobi offers great difficulties of drainage and it will be hard ever to make it satisfactory from a sanitary point of view".

Whitehouse remained undeterred and firmly believed that in time his railway base would attract a nucleus of traders for the infant commercial enterprises, then still in the planning stages. Suitable or not, Nairobi was ultimately to become the largest concentration of population in the eastern half of Africa between Cairo and Johannesburg.

Nairobi did have one great advantage for the railway builders. Unlike the semi-desert wastes which the line had passed through on its way up from the coast, the country around the capital was fairly well-populated. It was just beyond the limits of Ukambani, where the Kamba people lived, and lay on the border between Maasailand and the country of the Kikuyu, the largest of Kenya's tribes.

While the Maasai preferred the open plains and the vast stretches of grassland for their precious cattle, the Kikuyu were forest dwellers and their lifestyle, as well as their mode of warfare, was dictated largely by the confines of the dense montane forests, extensive clumps of bamboo and other thickets. Essentially cultivators, the Kikuyu made good use of their fertile land, well-watered soil and equable climate to grow a variety of food crops. These included sweet potatoes, yams and cassava which survived even drought years, as well as maize, bananas, beans and sugar cane which thrived in the wetter years.

At the turn of the century, just when the tiny township of Nairobi was beginning to expand, there were growing demands for food, not only from the urban population, but also from the large numbers of workers along the railway line. Unfortunately, this coincided with a period of prolonged drought which had turned much of the countryside into a disaster area. With it, famine took a heavy toll of the people especially the Maasai. The food shortage was worsened by serious outbreaks of fatal cattle sicknesses. These natural disasters also hit the Wakamba, and their plight was made worse by a smallpox epidemic. Although Maasai cattle had been decimated by the cattle diseases, much of the Kikuyu country miraculously remained unaffected by the ravages, and food was still fairly plentiful. One writer later called Kikuyu land at that time "a supermarket in a boneyard".

This was providential for the new arrivals settling in Nairobi and the surrounding area, including those building the difficult railway alignment up the Kikuyu Escarpment. So many demands were made on the Kikuyu for food by the many caravans crossing their land on the way to Uganda that they became reluctant to sell to foreigners. Some of them also began to fear the effects of the railway's arrival on their future lives, and were openly hostile to what they regarded as a dangerous and mushrooming intrusion.

Without local food supplies things would have become very serious for the railway construction operations in the vicinity. By this time the number of Indian labourers had increased considerably and their daily ration intake was about 21 tons – much of it rice and wheat flour which had to be imported and then railed up to Nairobi. This left little space on the trains for other food, so there was a pressing need for large amounts of local produce to feed the other people working for the railway, as well as the Government employees creating the new capital rising out of the papyrus swamps.

Preceding pages: Canadian-built '92 Class' diesel labouring up the eastern wall of the Rift escarpment with heavy goods train. The dormant Longonot volcano, makes an impressive background for this 1,500-foot (460m) ascent.

Above: Florence Preston, wife of construction boss Robert O. Preston, hammers home the last key of the 580-mile long (930 kms) track on the shores of Lake Victoria on 20 December 1901.

Above: Preston overcame the barrier of the Rift's steep wall by improvising a temporary cable railway to lower locomotives and wagons directly down the slope — while work continued on the gradual descent of the main line to the valley floor. This saved valuable months as platelayers could move up the Rift Valley with the track.

Left: One of the early 'N Class' locomotives which first worked the new line hauling an inspection train at Limuru near the edge of the Great Rift Valley.

Fortunately, a British ex-soldier had already cultivated cordial relations with the Kikuyu and had built up a thriving business with them. This was John Boyes, who called himself "The King of the Wa-Kikuyu", an adventurer, and former trooper in the war against the Matabele in Rhodesia. In 1898 he moved north to Kenya and began trading in ivory and other local commodities despite obstacles placed in his way by British officials who were discouraging white entrepreneurs, whom they saw as a possible aggravation to the local people.

Boyes first secured contracts to supply food to the British troops sent to help quell a serious mutiny by Sudanese soldiers working for the British in Uganda. As time went on he formed closer relations with many Kikuyu chiefs who were impressed by his bluster and assertiveness. Like Joseph Thomson, he was not above guile and deception in his dealings with

Above: Highest point of any railway in the Commonwealth — Timboroa Summit — at 9,136 feet (2784m) above sea level in the Kenya highlands on the direct line to Uganda built in the 1920s. The original line, which goes to Lake Victoria via Mau Summit, crests a maximum height of 8,379 feet (2553m).

Above: Canadian-built '92 Class' diesel locomotive in the original green and yellow livery of the old E.A.R.&H. system emerging from Limuru Tunnel before the start of the long drop into the Great Rift Valley.

Africans. For instance, he told one chief that white men were "unkillable", then proceeded to shoot a solid rifle cartridge right through a nearby tree. The Kikuyu were further impressed when Boyes told them that if they went to a distant mountain, they would find the same bullet had gone right through that as well! But the Kikuyu did not remain gullible for long.

Boyes also ran into serious trouble with the strict colonial administrators, especially when he helped some of his Kikuyu friends fight a battle against a group of rival Kikuyu. His enterprise was irrepressible and eventually Boyes had whole teams of Kikuyu porters delivering quantities of food to the railway work force at distant points along the rail route. His attempt to use donkeys eventually failed when the dreaded tsetse flies killed off the animals.

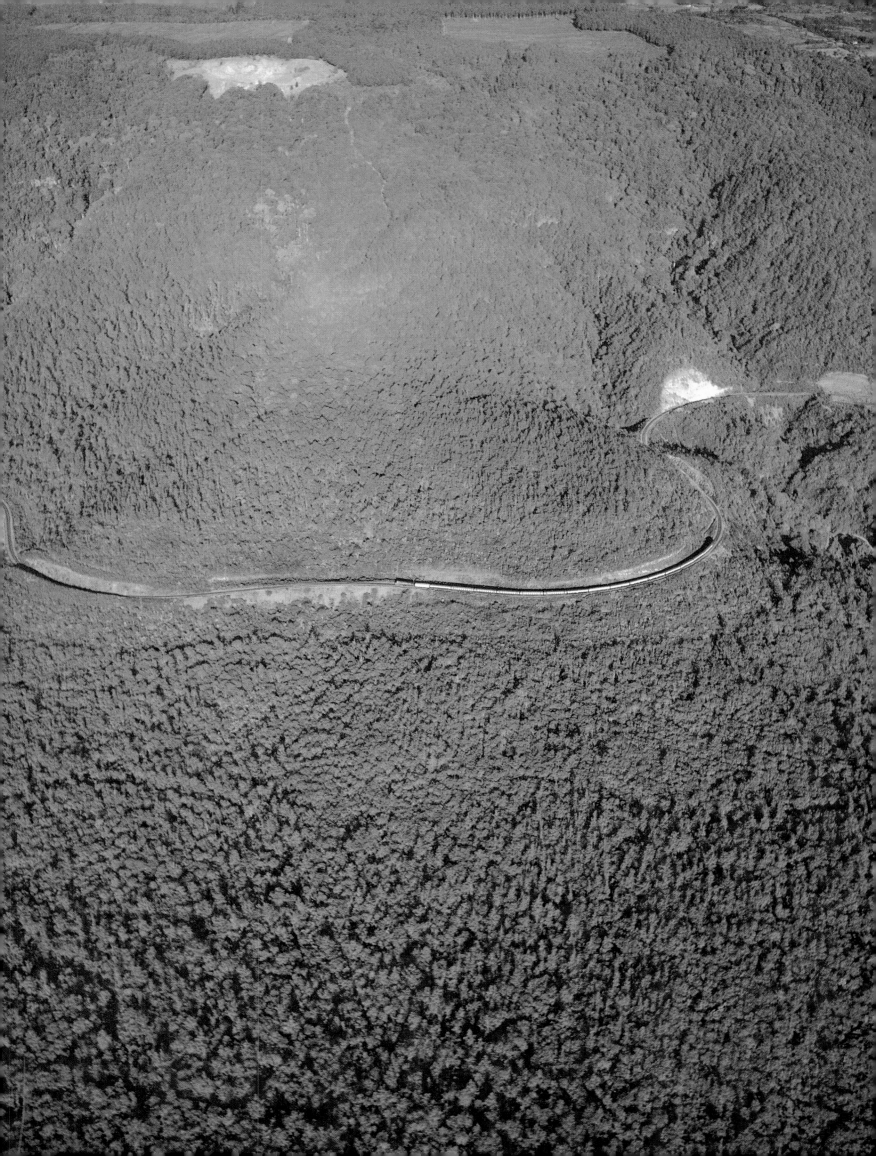

Opposite: Twisting sinuously, a long passenger train negotiates one of the many sharp curves on the descent of the eastern Rift Valley wall.

In the highlands beyond Nairobi the railway gangs revelled in the cool climate and green landscape, lush contrast to the sun-scorched lowlands. As the platelaying gangs were now well out of the game country, morale was high with the knowledge that no more man-eating lions were prowling around the camps at night. There had been other incidents with wild animals on the plains before reaching Nairobi, notably when one large bull rhinoceros persistently charged a locomotive. It almost derailed the engine until the enraged beast was killed by a well-placed rifle shot.

Once beyond Limuru almost 8,000 feet (2,440 m) above sea level, the engineers and labourers braced themselves for the steep descent into the Rift Valley. Due to the incessant pressure from London for speed, temporary tracks had to be laid round some of the major obstacles and an unorthodox scheme was then devised to lay the line down to the valley floor as quickly as possible. The plan initially involved constructing a gradual descent over a stretch of 10 miles (16 kms), by building a number of viaducts to preserve a constant gradient, but as Preston realized that this would take some time to complete and seriously delay the permanent track reaching the foot of the escarpment, he improvised a type of "cliff railway" which lowered wagons and even locomotives directly down the steep slopes with a rope and pulley attachment, as used on mountain cable cars. One observer likened it to a "ski slope". Altogether the line dropped 2,000 feet (610 m).

For Preston's "direct drop", a wide-gauge track was laid down the slope with four different gradients or angles of incline, two of them with double tracks so that a descending laden platform would be slowed by the counter-weight of another platform coming up with an empty wagon. These two steep inclines, both at an angle of 45 degrees, meant that the locomotives and rolling stock had to be lowered on flatcars, each of which had their outfacing front wheels 10 feet (3 m) below the rear wheels, so as to provide a level surface.

The gauge on which these flatcars operated was 5ft 6ins (1.67 m) and they were raised and lowered by steampowered winches. Precarious though the contraption was, it worked well as a temporary expedient. Its main advantage was that it enabled bulk supplies to be lowered to the valley floor so that work could begin on track-laying further ahead.

The slower building of the viaducts for the permanent alignment went on at the same time. The "funicular" also enabled some locomotives and wagons to be lowered for use at the railhead as it moved ahead across the valley floor. This engineering ingenuity provided quite a spectacle in the heart of Africa – more so early in 1900 when it went into full operation.

Above: After the tortuous descent of the Escarpment wall the track straightens as it reaches the floor of the Rift Valley near Naivasha.

Overleaf: The narrow metre-gauge track permitted
sharper curves to be laid to negotiate difficult terrain.

77

*Above: Dropping more than 4,600 feet (1420m) in
only 90 miles, the line from the Mau Summit to Lake
Victoria crosses a long viaduct.*

There had been some delay in the arrival of the winch gear and the special
flatcars, but all were in place and working order when the drought ended
and heavy rains began to saturate the slopes of the Rift Valley. This made
work extremely difficult and dangerous but, principally through Preston's
enterprise, not a single worker was killed during the construction. The
"funicular" operated for 18 months before the permanent track reached
the valley floor and was linked up to the tracks already laid down. It was
then abandoned.

The combination of Whitehouse's foresight and Preston's ingenuity
resulted in much time saving and put the Uganda Railway 170 miles (272
kms) ahead of where it would have been had track-laying been held up
until all the viaducts were completed.

But then the Uganda Railway ran into a major financial problem. All its funds were exhausted. The Railway Committee members were forced to go, cap in hand, to Parliament to seek an extra £2 million – an amount which brought the total cost of the railway up to £5 million, way above the original estimate based on MacDonald's perfunctory preliminary survey. The revised bill was remarkably close to Henry Labouchere's cost projection during the earlier House of Commons debate, when he criticised the construction of the "Lunatic Line".

The Committee's appeal was too good an opportunity for Labouchere to let it go by unnoticed. In his usual barbed manner, he declared "…if ever again we intend to make a railway in any part of Africa, the very last men we should put at the head of it is a committee of Foreign Office clerks". In the end, Parliament was forced to insist on even greater economies in construction, but not at the expense of speed which remained, as ever, the top priority.

Above: Curved viaduct spans rich farmlands near Molo through which the Nakuru-Kisumu line passes. Many of these were built originally of timber to speed up construction, but were later converted into steel structures.

Overleaf: Extensive marshalling yards and rail workshops in heart of Nairobi with the 'Y' rail formation (just below centre of picture) devised as a simpler method of turning locomotives than installing costly turntable.

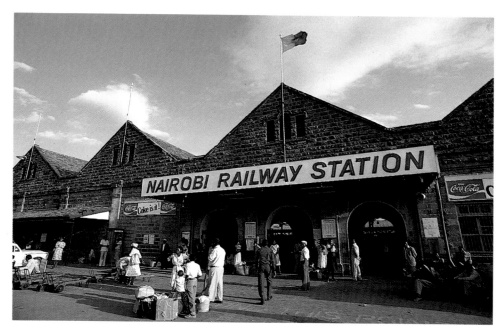

Above: Imposing stone facade of the Kenya Railway headquarters in Nairobi built around 1928. For a time it also served as the Headquarters for the amalgamated E.A.R.&H. system.

Above right: Entrance to Nairobi Railway Station has changed little since railhead reached the desolate swamp which became Kenya's capital on 30 May 1899.

With all this pressure, it was a lucky break for Whitehouse and his team when an advance survey party made an important discovery which would shorten the line to the Lake by nearly 100 miles (160 kms). A Mr Blackett, whose initials have been lost in the mists of time, found the 'short-cut' on the original alignment, and to mark his discovery a flat-topped mountain alongside the new route near Londiani was re-named 'Mount Blackett'. This route went out of Nakuru, ascending the Rift Valley's western wall known as the Mau Escarpment, then by way of Njoro, Molo and Elburgon to Mau Summit. From there it was a gentle gradient down to the shores of Lake Victoria.

Although more tortuous – and with sharper curves than on Captain MacDonald's original alignment – the Blackett route passed through a temperate, high-altitude zone around Molo which offered great potential for farming and rearing sheep. (MacDonald's proposed line climbed out of the Rift Valley near Eldama Ravine, then twisted its way upward to open savannah country on the Uasin Gishu Plateau. Then, after traversing this plain, also very suitable for agriculture, his route veered south-west and down the valley of the Nzoia River to a terminus at Port Victoria. Much later, in the 1920s, the MacDonald plan was revived and used as the alignment for a new direct rail link to Uganda.)

In place of Port Victoria on the shore of the main lake, the terminus was now located 60 miles (96 kms) to the east – at the head of the Kavirondo or Winam Gulf, where today Kisumu stands. It had the merit of being much closer to Mombasa and this reduced construction costs considerably.

Before he finally accepted this major alteration in the original rail route however Whitehouse, true to type, first insisted on surveying the new area to consider the practicability of the alignment.

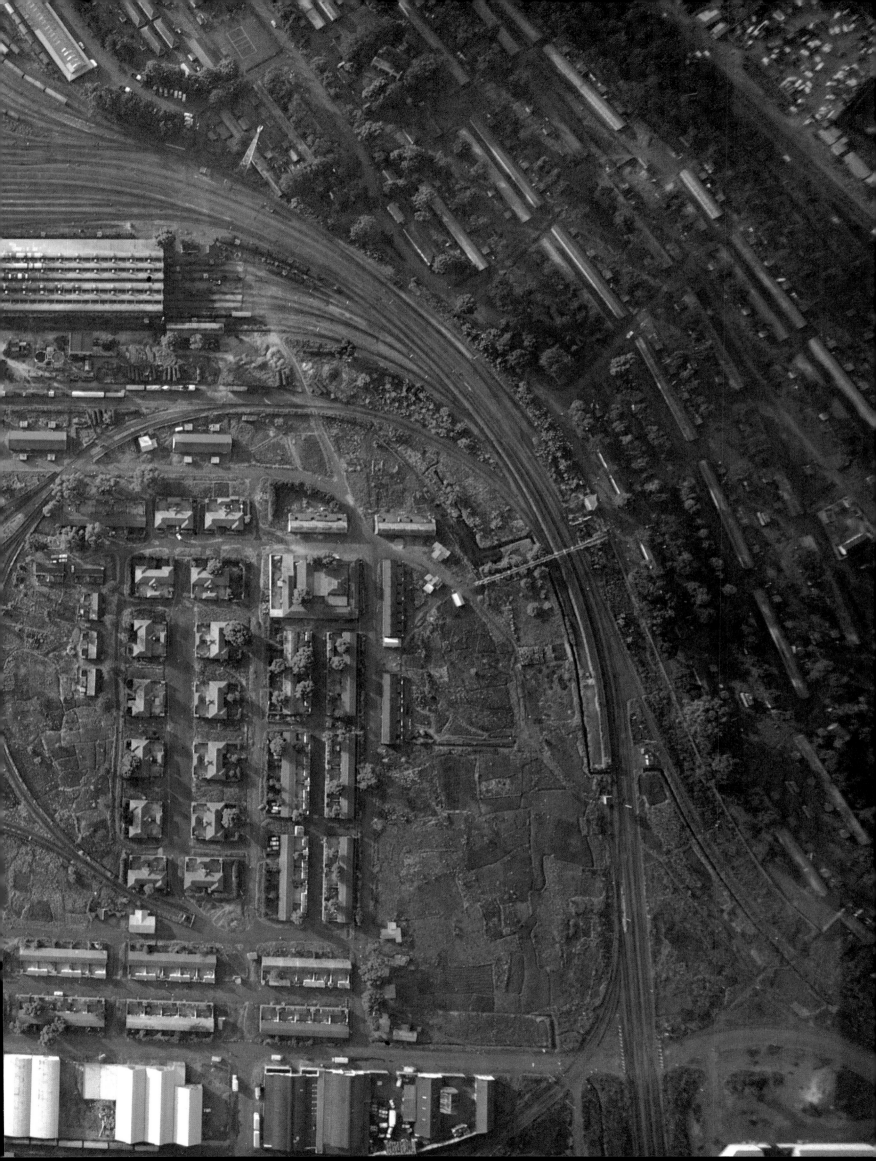

Below: Section of the Nairobi goods marshalling yard with the main station to the left of centre and Nairobi skyline in background.

This meant an 800 mile (1,287 kms) march through hitherto unexplored and trackless terrain. He reckoned then that as much as 114 miles (182 kms) could be saved, but when the track was eventually laid, the difference proved to be only 74 miles (119 kms)– but still a great saving both in time and materials.

There were numerous misfortunes and delays before the Uganda Railway was able to proceed beyond Nakuru and for a time the "end of the line" was at the western end of Nakuru Railway Station. Early photographs show the scene graphically as if the bare and mysterious land beyond was forbidden territory. One major delay was caused by a strike of British junior staff in Mombasa, which spread up the tracks to other ranks of employees before it was settled.

The climb up the Mau Escarpment proved less of an engineering challenge than the descent of the eastern wall of the Rift Valley. But it was still not easy. About 1,000 tons of rails were dumped at the railhead beyond Nakuru. From there they had to be manhandled some 10 miles (16 kms) to a height of 8,700 feet (2,652 m), to the final stretch over the Mau Summit.

During the ascent, which entailed many sharp curves, 27 viaducts had to be built. As was standard practice on this railway, the initial ones were made of local timber, later replaced with steel imported from the United States. The originals were of the trestle type, some quite high.

Finally, the railway reached its highest point at Mau Summit. At that point, cold, wet weather made working conditions difficult and train derailments were frequent. The rails tended to sag over the swampy ground, with the locomotives leaving the line and bogging down in the mud.

Without a mobile crane, it was far from easy to haul them back on the tracks – but, ingenious as usual, Preston fitted the locos with buffer beams in front of the engines only a few inches above the rails.

These beams prevented the locos ploughing too deep into the mire after derailment, and a few hefty heaves with crowbars were sufficient to get them back on the rails.

After Mau Summit came the final 100 mile stretch (160 kms), all of it downhill, past Londiani and Blackett's mountain. Conditions way up at 9,000 feet (2,743 m) on the Summit were very severe, especially for "lowland" Indian labourers unaccustomed to the cold and damp. The Pathans and other hill-tribes were less affected. There were times at night when water froze in buckets and icy sleet would cover the ground with a white mantle – only a stone's throw from the Equator. At other times the rain would turn the ground into a quagmire, holding up track-laying until it could be drained off.

86

Above: Diesel locos in the ageing, smoke-blackened sheds which once housed the leviathans of East Africa's steam age.

With drier weather again, the going improved – but more trouble lay just ahead. While no firm deadline had ever been laid down for completing the railway, the engineers had targetted their arrival at the lake terminus for 1 January, 1902. But they had not reckoned on the Nandi tribe which inhabited the forest heights overlooking the railway as it twisted downwards from the Mau. The Nandi had already shown their resentment against the line's "intrusion" by staging several raids. Now they were attracted by the miles and miles of copper wire in the telegraph line running alongside the railway, which they coveted for ornamental bracelets. The rails themselves and other metal bars were considered "just the thing" for making spears and other weapons of war, and so their raids became more frequent and more forceful.

In explaining to the people back in Britain why the Nandi were constantly raiding the railway, Sir Charles Eliot, the Commissioner for the East Africa Protectorate, wrote: "One can imagine what thefts would be committed on a European railway if the telegraph wires were pearl necklaces and the rails first-rate sporting guns, and it is not surprising that the Nandi yielded to the temptation."

Their biggest haul of loot was seized even before the railway reached their territory. This consisted of several sections of the boat 'William Mackinnon', due to be launched on Lake Victoria. It had been carried much of the way from the coast by porters in 60 pound loads. When the pieces were reassembled at Port Florence in mid-1900, a number of essential parts for its boiler were missing – in the hands of the Nandi. It was several months before replacement parts arrived from Britain, and the boat could be launched.

Before the railway appeared on the scene, the Nandi had shown their warlike tendencies to Uganda-bound caravans. They saw their passage as an excuse to exact tribute in the form of a share of the cargo the caravans carried. Some time before, the British had built a fort at Eldama Ravine to serve as a base for the Sudanese troops brought from Uganda, but they mutinied over rates of pay and other issues, deserted and made their way back to their homes in the Sudan.

Once they left, the British were faced with the problem of finding other troops to keep the Nandi in check, but this took time, and as the railway tracks approached in 1900, the Nandi were again on the rampage, menacing their neighbours and pillaging travellers' caravans. The railway remained a convenient source of loot for the Nandi warriors after that.

On top of all this, the Indian labourers had become an indisciplined, unruly mob, their camps notorious as dens of vice which disgusted the Africans who witnessed it.

Opposite: Nairobi rail workshops formed the first major engineering complex in East Africa and became the forerunner of Kenya's modern industrial base.

Above: Foundryman casting new brake shoes to replace those worn down on constant curves and gradients.

The Nandi chiefs were outraged by the liberties taken with their women and girls. Charles Miller wrote in 'The Lunatic Express': "It must be said that Nandi interference with the line was not animated solely by greed and xenophobia. Hostility to the white man's railway was exarcerbated by the behaviour of brown men, who laid not only the tracks but also every Nandi girl and boy they could lure into their tents."

British officials constantly remonstrated with the railway management about the lax discipline and for closing their eyes to what went on in the Indians' camps. A senior British Army officer, Sir Frederick Jackson, called them "sinks of iniquity" and chiefs of the neighbouring Kipsigis tribe joined with the Nandi in objecting strongly to the behaviour of railway workers. In spite of their sympathies with such complaints, however, British officials were determined to restrain the Nandi from exacting revenge by pillage and murder, so they made plans to bring in a large force to deal with the Nandi reprisal attacks.

This punitive expedition proved a failure. Contingents of Sudanese and Indian troops were ambushed with heavy losses, after which a full-scale military campaign was unleashed on the Nandi by the Special Commissioner in Uganda, Sir Harry Johnston. He issued his order just as Preston was starting to lay the railway tracks down the western side of the Mau towards the lake.

The invasion was abruptly called off at the last moment on the orders of a top Foreign Office man from London, Sir Clement Hill, who happened to be in Kenya at the time, inspecting progress on the railway in his other capacity as a Railway Commissioner. He was most anxious for the construction to move ahead as fast as possible and ruled out a war with the Nandi because of the delay this would inevitably cause.

Infuriated by having his orders countermanded, Johnston accused Hill of "appeasement" and a heated argument developed between them. But the effect of this row was for the British administration to restrain the Nandi temporarily so that rail construction work could continue without hindrance from further raids. Preston hurried on with his platelaying, avoiding any natural obstacles. He even built a temporary diversion around the only tunnel on the line while the blasting was still in progress.

By the middle of 1900 the railway had reached the flat plains at the foot of the Nandi Escarpment, near Muhoroni, only 35 miles (56 kms) from its destination. Only one more intervening station, Kibigori, was planned before the lake terminus and Preston delivered a "pep talk" calling on his workers for one last superhuman effort to beat the end-of-year deadline. The men immediately responded – so much so that the tracks raced ahead of the telegraph line. Kibigori was passed and at Kibos the construction gang could actually see the lake.

Opposite: Sad relic of the steam age — a 'Tribal Class' engine named after one of East Africa's colourful ethnic groups — lies rusting in Nairobi marshalling yards.

Opposite: Another 'Tribal Class' loco decays beneath a collapsing roof in a forgotten corner of the old loco sheds at Mombasa.

Then came trouble. First a wave of dysentery laid many low, only for them to fall victims later to virulent malaria. Torrential rains then broke, dissolving the earth embankments as if they were built of sugar. The railway track turned into a sea of slime, so sodden that the locomotives dare not stop lest, together with the rails, they sank into the morass. At this low ebb in the fortunes of the construction workers, the Nandi launched another devastating raid, dashing down from their rocky hiding places above the railway, spears gleaming above their bright-painted shields, terrorising the defenceless Indian labourers. They were unable to summon help as the telegraph line was still far behind, the Nandi raiders having filched every inch of copper wire remaining for the extension to the railhead.

All the panic-stricken Indians could do was to keep out of the way as the raiders plundered the railway stores. So excited were the Nandi with their latest loot that they did not attack the workers.

One direct result of the plunder of the wire for the telegraph line was a tragic rail accident in the final days of the epic construction. It was solely due to the lack of communication between stations in the final section before the terminus that two engines collided head on as they travelled along the single track. Two White drivers were killed.

But at last the dark days were over. The Nandi had retreated into their uplands, the fevers abated and the workers were all back at their jobs, pushing on over the last remaining miles.

On Friday 20 December 1901, the historic moment arrived with Florence Preston, on the site of the new port named after her, driving in the last key of the last rail, watched by her husband, three railway officials – and a dog.

Five years and four months after it was started, the completed 'Lunatic Line', a single metre-gauge track which snaked its way for 581 miles (930 kms) over deserts, rivers and mountains became the most important single development "tool" in the history of East Africa.

In the words of a contemporary British author, this was "the most courageous railway in the world." At that time – at £9,500 sterling per mile – it was probably also the most expensive railway in the world.

Although the Uganda railway had reached its terminus by the lake shore a few days ahead of schedule, many months elapsed before the final alignments and subsidiary works were completed.

Once the trains reached Port Florence, work began in earnest to develop the port as a base for steamer traffic on the lake. Several ships were railed up in sections to join the lone 'William Mackinnon', which had been plying the lake waters since its launch in 1900. First to arrive in 1903 was the 700-ton 'Winifred,' followed a year later by her sister ship the 'Sybil.' Their main function was to shuttle between the railhead and the Ugandan ports of Jinja, Port Bell and Entebbe. A later arrival was the 1,100-ton 'Clement Hill' in 1906.

Whereas speed of construction had been the top priority dictated from London, the emphasis now switched to finding enough local goods for the railway to carry and make the venture pay its way. The Government in London was still under strong attack from its critics over the high cost of the line and felt compelled to show a profit as soon as possible.

But there was very little freight to carry. Some cotton was available in Uganda for shipment to markets in Europe, but most of the route along which the railway passed was an economic desert.

Anxious to please his masters in London, the British Special Commissioner for East Africa, Sir Charles Eliot, began looking around for possible cargoes soon after his arrival in 1900, but the country in general was sparsely populated and although he foresaw immense possibilities for agricultural export, Sir Charles was doubtful whether the local people were capable of developing an export market of any size.

Apart from a small amount of maize, Eliot felt there was nothing the agricultural tribes grew which the world wanted and he dismissed the abundant hides and skins provided by the nomadic pastoralists as "almost useless".

Only by encouraging white settlers to farm in the fertile highlands, Eliot decided, could the Uganda Railway and the country it traversed be saved from "economic stagnation". Outrageous and unabashedly racist though his views might seem today, Eliot's recommendations that white emigrants should be enticed to settle in Kenya were accepted at the time without question by the British Foreign Office. His chief justification for his proposal was that such fertile land should go only to those who could turn it to the greatest productivity. Arguing that so long as industrialised countries needed agricultural produce, he said it was inevitable that this demand should be met. To lock up any productive regions of the world purely in the interests of a tiny group of inhabitants constituted a "crime against humanity as a whole", claimed Eliot.

Emphasising that some 200 miles (320 kms) of the rail route between Nairobi and Lake Victoria urgently needed to be developed for farming, he blandly asserted that the local people cultivating such land were unable to produce any surplus food. He even wrote: "The whole idea of producing a surplus is foreign to the native mind. It has never occurred to them to do so: for centuries there has been no market for it but rats."

Preceding pages: The early Uganda Railway did much to open up the interior of Kenya and Uganda for agricultural and mineral exploitation. This branch line down into the Rift Valley and Lake Magadi gave access to profitable mineral deposits, especially soda ash.

Opposite: Besides maize and wheat from the Kenya highlands, the main cargo carried by the railway to Mombasa for export was Uganda cotton. Bales were shipped across Lake Victoria from Jinja and Port Bell to the Kisumu railhead.

Below: Early derailment — one of many in the early days. Most of these were caused by heavy rainstorms which washed away the track or put it out of alignment.

Below right: Nairobi Station, in the early 1900s, with rickshaws and porters awaiting the arrival of the Mombasa train.

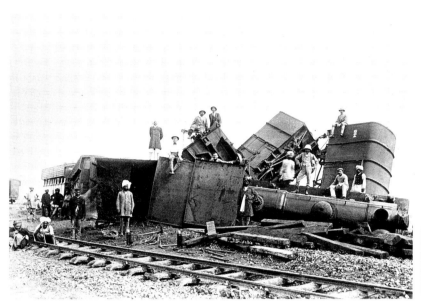

Eliot also defended his settlement plan by stating: "We are not destroying any old or interesting system, but simply introducing order into bleak, uninteresting, brutal barbarism." His views were apparently shared to some extent by the Secretary of State for the Colonies, Mr Joseph Chamberlain, who had travelled on the Uganda Railway. After a brief glimpse of the country through the train windows, he forecast that its future prosperity would depend upon exports of wheat and wool.

A more seasoned but lesser official, John Ainsworth, who had served with the IBEA as its agent in Ukamba, took a more enlightened view of the local populations' abilities, and when he arrived in Kisumu in 1907 as Provincial Commissioner for Nyanza, he launched a drive among the local Luo people and their Luhya neighbours to find out if they could provide some freight for the new railway.

Above left: Both Winston Churchill (1907) and ex-US President Theodore Roosevelt (1909) rode the Uganda Railway in adventurous fashion — at the front seated above the cow-catcher. Roosevelt, on left of picture, brought a large retinue with him — and killed vast numbers of wildlife, including more than a dozen rhino.

Above: Britain's Prince of Wales (left) rides the railway during his East Africa tour in 1928.

Opposite: Trains from Magadi reach the main line to Mombasa at Konza.

Overleaf: Double-headed for the steep haul up from the Rift Valley floor, a train laden with soda ash pulls out of Magadi on its way to Mombasa. The pinkish deposit in the foreground is the trona from which the soda ash is harvested.

Opposite: Group of Maasai in a variety of clothing from a tribal 'shuka' to jeans hurry to board the guard's van of a slow-moving train in Maasailand.

Above: Goods train on the Taveta branch line from Voi, which connects the Kenya system with the Tanga line, waits for road traffic to pass over a level crossing.

Opposite: Young Maasai warriors try their skill at drilling a hole in a newly-laid sleeper on the Magadi line.

At that time the infant line was still in desperate need of goods of any description to carry for export, but the only cargoes offered locally were either cotton from Uganda, which had to be shipped across the lake, or produce from the German territory to the south and south-west.

Ainsworth encouraged local people to drain lakeside swamps by assuring them that not only would this check the breeding-rate of the troublesome malaria-carrying mosquitoes, but also provide good land on which to grow food. Many responded and soon Ainsworth was able to write home that he had "a wonderful asset in the native people". His gentle persuasion did indeed pay off. Four years later, as he was about to leave on transfer, Ainsworth was able to record that Nyanza Province, or Kavirondo as it was then called, had exported £44,000 worth of farm produce on the railway. Within two years the Kavirondo area had become the railway's best customer – although earlier on it had been totally "written off" as incapable of exporting anything. This success encouraged the authorities to plan an extension of the rails from the Port Florence terminus to Butere, although it did not, in fact, materialise until 20 years later.

Meanwhile Eliot lost no time in pushing ahead with his plans to turn over large tracts of what he judged to be vacant or uncultivated land to White immigrants. In 1902, to avoid possible complications with the local rulers in Uganda, he detached the entire eastern part of the Uganda Protectorate and merged it with the East Africa Protectorate, in the process roughly demarcating the present frontiers of Kenya. By this move, the Uganda Railway's terminus at Kisumu now fell inside Kenya, with the new Uganda border some 53 miles (85 kms) to the west.

Provisions for land grants to White settlers were soon made, based on laws derived mainly from Canada, with an addition from a Cyprus law which prohibited the keeping of goats! On first application a new arrival would be allocated 160 acres (64.5 ha) of land free, and if he developed the land properly, would be eligible for three more similar acreages to a maximum of one square mile. The new law also provided for settlers to purchase land up to a maximum of 1,000 acres (405 ha). One of the takers was Lord Delamere, who first set eyes on the embryo railway at Tsavo in 1898 as he was heading for the coast *en route* to Britain. He immediately booked passage back from England when he heard of Eliot's land scheme. Arriving in Nairobi on the twice-weekly train from Mombasa in January, 1903, he found the new town with a railway station in use, albeit little more than a single platform with a few strips of tin roofing overhead and a kitchen clock to show the time.

The English aristocrat was soon to become the infant colony's leading settler and fiery champion of the White cause. It was not long before he acquired large stretches of land in the highlands, including the 100,000-acre (4,047 ha) "Equator Ranch" near the railway at Njoro, beyond Nakuru. Many others were also acquiring land in accordance with the Government's policy to offer farm plots to white immigrants alongside the railway line so that in time their produce would be conveniently exported through Mombasa to overseas markets. Later the construction of several branch lines to the north of the main line enabled the Government to use this policy to give over much greater acreage to White farmers, thus creating the racially-exclusive "White Highlands" which became a major bone of contention before Kenya became free and independent.

Potatoes were the first crop to be grown in quantity by the newly-arrived white farmers, then came maize, beans, ground nuts, plus some rice, rubber and tobacco. Later, what was to become a highly-lucrative crop, coffee, was introduced by missionaries at St. Austin's, near Nairobi, followed by wheat, fruit and vegetables. Much later the profitable tea plantations were started.

It was in 1905 that the Uganda Railway reported its first profitable year with "up" traffic to Nairobi and beyond amounting to over 15,000 tons of imports, three times higher than in the year before. "Down" exports amounted to 8,258 tons, which was more than 2,500 tons above the previous year. Passenger traffic to Nairobi was much heavier than in the other direction, due to the ever-growing number of immigrants arriving at Mombasa.

Above: Wrought-iron initials at base of seat frame — UR — signifies venerable service at a Kenya wayside halt.

The new railway had an even greater impact on Uganda, as it reduced the time of a journey to the coast from this land-locked country from three months to a mere six days. Its luxury exports, such as ivory, could easily stand the much higher transport charges on the railway, compared with carriage by porters, since a ton of ivory fetched anything from £130 to £190 overseas.

Farmers growing coffee or cotton found the railway charges somewhat steep compared with the world prices paid for those commodities. At that time the tariff was £2.50 per ton for goods from Uganda to the coast. However, one of the countries where Kenya found a ready market was South Africa, and the tariff from Nairobi to South African ports was only £3 a ton.

Besides acquiring farms in the best areas, and on some poor land as well, Lord Delamere was also busy writing to prospective settlers around the world urging them to take up offers of free land, which he described as far better than in Australia or New Zealand. At first they were slow in coming and the authorities worried that, despite all the publicity for free land, very few seemed anxious to migrate from Britain or other Commonwealth states.

In 1908 a second wave of white immigrants began to arrive, some to settle on the edge of Kikuyu country north of Nairobi where coffee and sisal plantations were being developed. Many more came to Kenya from South Africa, the result of a "recruiting mission" which Eliot sent off south to encourage white farmers to migrate from there, especially those who had become disillusioned over the outcome of the South African War.

Inevitably, complaints arose over the rates charged by the railway, and also on its management policy. On the one hand, the British Treasury insisted that the Uganda Railway had been built solely for making a profit and this did not take into account the economic interests of the country itself. On the other hand, white settlers argued that not only was it a commercial railway system, but it was also part of the Protectorate's production cycle – a vital link in the farm-to-consumer chain of ploughing, planting, harvesting, grading, packing, transporting and finally marketing. Eliot tended to side with the settlers in this dispute.

"There seems a tendency to treat the railway as something apart, built in the air, so to speak, and independent of terrestrial things," he wrote. "It is the backbone of the East Africa Protectorate, but a backbone is as useless without a body as a body is without a backbone."

By this time the Railway was doing better every year, as more and more export crops were carried down to Mombasa. Thoughts then turned to constructing branch lines to reach some of the more remote farming land. In 1909, a new Governor arrived, Sir Percy Girouard, a man with a passion for building railways. He was soon lobbying for branch lines, including a spur from Nairobi towards the slopes of Mount Kenya to serve the coffee estates and fruit farms beyond Thika.

Below: Dinner gong used by restaurant car stewards.

Middle: Early typewriter used by Sir George Whitehouse.

Bottom: Number plates from locos sent for scrap.

He was already aware of the parsimony of the Government in London, having just come from Nigeria where he had supervised the building of a railway to Kano in the far north. He reasoned that his request for money to build a branch line in Kenya would be rejected out of hand by the Treasury, whereas they might look more favourably on a "tramway" which could be a "light railway", costing only £2,500 a mile, compared with £9,500 a mile for the much heavier main line.

The ruse succeeded, and work duly started on the 'Thika Tramway' in 1912, the Protectorate having been allowed to float its first loan after the railway itself had come to the rescue when the Protectorate Administration faced a financial crisis. With its profits rising 600 per cent in four years, the railway had enough money to bail out the Protectorate from its deficit situation.

The 30 mile (40 kms) track to Thika was to be the start of a far longer branch railway which twisted through the Kikuyu farmland past Fort Hall and Nyeri to terminate on the lower slopes of Mount Kenya at Nanyuki, on the edge of the great Laikipia Plateau. But it was not until 1930 that the entire route was completed. Inevitably, it was nothing so simple as a tramway, except that the rails were lighter than the Uganda Railway track and instead of importing labourers for the platelaying, the work was carried out by the Government Public Works Department – at times with forced labour.

Meanwhile in Uganda, far removed from any linking network, construction had started in 1911 on a small link line which bore the grand name of the 'Busoga Railway'. It extended for almost 50 miles (80 kms) from the Lake Victoria port town of Jinja to Namasagali, on Lake Kioga, running northwards almost parallel to the Victoria (White) Nile. When opened in 1913, it served a new steamer service which had been introduced on the weed-choked lake by two paddle steamers, the 'Speke' and the 'Stanley'. An even shorter line was also constructed in Uganda at about the same time, linking Port Bell with Kampala, six miles (9.5 kms) away.

All further rail construction and improvement work ceased in East Africa once the First World War broke out, the only exception being a mineral branch from the Uganda Railway at Konza. It went down the steep escarpment to Lake Magadi, rich in soda ash, which was to prove valuable for glass-making and greatly helped the Allied war effort. This line also opened a convenient route to the almost inaccessible country south of Magadi which bordered on what was then the "enemy territory" of German East Africa.

Although far removed from the European theatre of war in 1914, East Africa was a battleground where British and German troops fought occasional set battles, but the conflict later developed into a protracted guerrilla operation. In this "bush-war" the German commander, General Paul Von Lettow-Vorbeck, fought a masterly rearguard action with a

108

Kenya Railways runs an annual competition for the best-kept station on its 1,656 mile (2,650km) system. A frequent winner is Naro Moru, left, on the lower slopes of Mt Kenya near the terminus of the branch line from Nairobi to Nanyuki and, above, it has plaques to show its commendable record.

mixed force of Germans and African *askaris*. He managed to evade capture by a large British pursuit force and was still at liberty when the war ended in 1918.

Right from the outbreak of hostilities, the Uganda Railway was a major target for attack as it was highly vulnerable, running for almost 200 miles (320 kms) more or less parallel with the frontier, but 50 miles (80 kms) to the north. Most of the terrain it ran through was sparsely populated and little but desert lay between the rails and the border, except for the massive bulk of Kilimanjaro, Africa's highest mountain.

All normal traffic came to a standstill. Orders had been given by the British military authorities that all locomotives operating between Nakuru and Kisumu should be concentrated at Nakuru, while those between Nairobi and Mombasa should remain in Nairobi. Those trains which did move by daylight were controlled by the military and carried either troops or military supplies.

Whether by intuition or good fortune, the Germans had built their Tanga Line with the Usambara and Pare mountain ranges between it and the border with the East Africa Protectorate, making it much more difficult for the British to mount attacks on that line. However, it was not long before German patrols launched hit-and-run raids on the exposed parts of the Uganda Railway, planting mines or blowing up bridges. Between 12 April, 1915, and 10 May, 1916, a total of 57 attempts were made to mine the railway, but vigilant patrols minimised the damage, especially by the East African Mounted Rifles, whose settler troopers knew the country well.

The very first attack in 1915 was an attempt to destroy a three-span bridge at Mile 218 from Mombasa, near Makindu, but the damage was quickly repaired. Altogether, locomotives and rolling stock were derailed 17 times in the early part of the war.

A patrol which tried to raid a station was beaten off and nine other patrols were intercepted before reaching the railway, including one which lost its way because its British map was inaccurate! In all, the tracks were damaged in 13 places.

Had it not been for the large amount of military traffic, the railway would have suffered disastrous losses during these war years, especially as the former major source of revenue dried up completely. This was cargo consigned to and from the German ports on Lake Victoria, such as Musoma, Mwanza and Bukoba. This traffic used to be routed via Port Florence, but ceased abruptly once the war started.

At the same time, however, the railway workshops in Nairobi soon became an efficient industrial plant, capable of metalwork of many kinds and proved a major asset to the Protectorate's war effort. An early contribution which took only ten days to construct, was an "armoured-train", consisting of a heavily-armoured engine and tender with two large bogie wagons fitted with armour plating to a height of six feet (1.8 m) above the wheels. Embrasures were cut out for rifles and mountings made for machine guns. There were powerful headlights fore and aft, with an additional searchlight fitted on one of the bogies. This was soon followed by a "hospital train" which the work shops made by gutting two old passenger coaches and adapting them for carrying wounded soldiers. The Nairobi workshops also handled a variety of smaller jobs for the military, ranging from mountings for naval guns to uniform buttons.

On the other side of the border, the Germans' agricultural research station, in the Usambara Mountains at Amani, proved remarkably versatile, making a radical switch to turning out munitions for the German troops.

The Uganda Railway then received a major boost at the end of 1915 when Britain decided to build a railway spur from Voi towards the German East Africa border at Taveta to support an offensive planned for the

following year. Taveta itself had been already taken by German troops and this small enclave had the distinction of being the only part of the British Empire occupied by the Germans in the First World War.

Construction on the line went on at a feverish pace and for a few months much of the traffic up from Mombasa consisted of wagons with track-laying materials.

Once the British military offensive got under way, the German forces began retreating from Moshi down the Tanga line to the sea. They were hotly pursued by the British forces, now under the command of General Jan Smuts, the South African war hero, later to become Prime Minister.

Meanwhile the military line was extended to Kahe, linking up to the Tanga line and Moshi. This was the first effort to connect the two countries by rail. Much later, it was torn up again on orders from London and only after a bitter row, during which Lord Delamere made a strong appeal in the House of Lords at Westminster, was this branch line rebuilt. It remains the only rail link between the Kenya-Uganda system and the German-built lines in present-day Tanzania.

Above: Twin light-duty '62 Class' diesels crossing bridge with a train of box cars on the Nanyuki branch line.

During the row, in 1924, the British Governor of Tanganyika opposed the rebuilding of the link-line, arguing that it would divert more traffic to the port of Mombasa, to the detriment of Tanga, which he hoped would become East Africa's third major port.

Eleven more stations were built to cope with the extra traffic on the Uganda Line and provide crossing points on the single line system to accommodate more and heavier trains. At this stage, "double-headed running" was introduced, with two locos coupled to one train to provide more power, especially on the gradients.

During these war years, the Uganda Railway also received a further much-needed consignment of 25 locomotives from India. They were by no means new and some were in urgent need of repair, but they did help to take the strain off the overworked but faithful veterans still in service.

The most serious problem hindering the smooth operation of the Railway up to 1920 was the difficulty of acquiring new locomotives, due mainly to a series of strikes in England, which held up work on the initial orders placed by the management in 1897 and 1898.

Only five new locos arrived in Mombasa on time, all of them "F" class, which did sterling work hauling trains over fairly long distances. But when the balance of 15 locos of this batch failed to arrive, the management had to turn to India to scrounge whatever they could among engines of the same metre-gauge which were in service only on certain lines. Many of those that India could spare were not only second-hand, but in the last stages of their useful lives, and were only kept running by sheer ingenuity. The deliveries included two "A" class engines, which proved so weak they could only haul newly-arrived railway material from the wharves to the railway storage yards.

Two others, of the "E" class, were more useful, with enough power to serve at the railhead as it moved ahead inland at the overall rate of around 100 miles (160 kms) a year (which was good as African railway construction went at the end of the 19th Century). Then, in 1899, India sent over six "N" class locomotives, distinguished by their extra-tall smokestacks and a 2-6-0 wheel arrangement. Twenty of them eventually went into service on the line and all performed exceptionally well, outlasting all the others, and were still railworthy when finally withdrawn in 1931.

Because of the rash of strikes at English engineering yards, the Uganda Railway authorities also turned to the United States for the next intake of locos. These arrived in 1900 – a total of 34 Baldwin-built "B" class 2-6-0 engines of about the same power as the old "F" class, even with similar cowcatchers in front.

Ultimately, a shipment of British-built "Mallets" arrived in Mombasa shortly before the First World War and this was a bold departure for the railway, since these were the first articulated locos put into service on the line and were much more powerful than the rest, with a tractive effort of 27,500 lbs – twice that of the "F"s and "B"s. (Some years before, the Germans introduced smaller "Malletts" on their Tanga Line.)

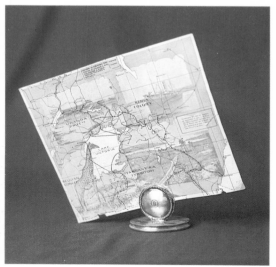

Opposite: Nostalgic re-creation of the early days of Kenya travel — refurbished Kenya Railways' vintage dining car — now by arrangement offers gourmet delights to modern rail enthusiasts on special 'sentimental safaris'.

Opposite: (bottom left) Silver coffee set, (centre) 1930s Railway menu, (right) Souvenir rail map of the 1930s.

Below: Old rail crests on egg-cups.

Middle: 'UR' cutlery set.

Bottom: Wine decanter and glass.

They were actually two engines in one, and certainly did the work of two of the older types, and had been designed especially for a light, narrow-gauge railway such as the Uganda Railway then was.

Although their added power proved a tremendous asset to the line, the "Mallets" were plagued with problems and some spent more time in the repair shops than in service. The main problem was caused by the firebars constantly burning out in the firebox grates. This defect puzzled engineers for a time. Eventually, they put it down to the fact that these engines had previously burned only on coal, as they had always been accustomed to using wood to fire the other engines.

The "Mallets" could not raise sufficient steam pressure on wood fires alone and conversion to oil-burning in wartime was out of the question. In the end, a compromise was reached – half wood and half coal – and went some way towards solving the problem.

By 1913, a total of 67 locomotives were in service on the Uganda Railway, which the General Manager in that year, Major H. B. Taylor used to call a "hill railway". He likened it to the narrow-gauge lines which led off the Indian State Railways' broader gauge tracks and wound their way up into the hills. But the Uganda Railway, though not built to handle heavy traffic at the outset, gradually developed into the main artery for commerce not only in Kenya, but also in Uganda and other countries beyond.

Its gauge was narrow (as compared to the "standard" gauge of 4ft 8.5ins – 1.5 m), the rails were light, varying from 50 to 80 lbs; and there were load restrictions on the line so that those designing locos for the Uganda Railway had to summon all their ingenuity to come up with engines that were compact, yet powerful enough to haul heavy loads up steep gradients.

At about the same time the "Mallets" reached the Protectorate, another newly-designed locomotive was also on its way. This was of a type already in use on the Assam-Bengal Railway – not articulated but a massive orthodox engine with a 4-8-0 wheel arrangement. This "G" class (later re-classified "EB") proved probably the most successful of all the early engines operating on the Uganda Railway. It did not have the tractive effort of the "Mallets", but worked magnificently hauling mail trains from Mombasa to Nairobi – although not beyond because of weight restrictions. Only seven were ordered, among them an improved version using superheated steam, and they remained in service from 1916 to 1934.

The arrival of these new engines made it possible for the management to introduce a daily service on the main line in 1920, as well as to haul up the soda ash from the Rift Valley floor at Lake Magadi.

Big development plans were in preparation, but first there had to be a major re-organisation of the management to cope with its new assets – shades of the days back in 1897 when its first "passengers" were troops *en route* to combat.

It had long been evident to the Railway's management that the single-line route to Lake Victoria, ending at Kisumu, was not the ideal means for linking Uganda with the sea. Moreover, in the hurry to get the original railway completed the decision to abandon MacDonald's original route from Nakuru up the Rift Valley's western wall at Eldama Ravine proved misguided in two respects.

The alternative Mau route, eventually selected, imposed severe limitations on traffic due to the very sharp curves, innumerable viaducts and steep gradients, averaging out at two per cent. As the inland terminus, Kisumu had proved a problem – its port and the entire Kavirondo (Winam) Gulf was much too shallow for ships with a normal draught. In this respect it lacked the advantage which the alternative port on the MacDonald route possessed and meant that if they continued to use Kisumu port as their base, essential to their operations, Lake Victoria ships would have to be very limited in size so as to maintain a shallow draught.

Three other surveys were conducted in the war years to look for an ideal route for the new branch of the Uganda Railway out of Nakuru and the consensus was to follow roughly the alignment originally proposed by MacDonald in 1891. This route was not only preferred because of its more gradual incline, but also for access to the Uasin Gishu. By 1920 this plateau was a highly-productive farming area, described later as "an ocean of cereals". In 1916, the line's General Manager wrote in his annual report: "The survey shows an alignment that is far more capable of working heavy traffic with ease than is possible on the Uganda Railway. The line will be 205 miles in length, with about seven miles of sidings and with a ruling grade of one and a half per cent, compensated with curvature, against an uncompensated grade of two percent on the parent line.

"With the possibility of the Uasin Gishu Railway in the future becoming the commencement of a trunk line to Uganda and the Congo, it is of importance that the most favourable conditions should be obtained, and on the alignment now obtained the tractive power can deal with a load one-third greater on the (new) Uganda line than it does on the (existing) Mau line between Fort Ternan and Nakuru."

Already the original 50 pound rails on the Mombasa to Nairobi sector were being replaced with 80 pound rails to carry the heavier traffic and it was likely that these heavier rails would also be used on the new route to Uganda.

However, the plans were to remain on paper for a few more years until construction began in the 1920s. In the interval, the settlers farming on the Uasin Gishu plateau and the adjoining Trans-Nzoia district had to endure a daunting and tenuous link with the rest of Kenya. This was a wagon trail through one quagmire after another in the dense forests of Timboroa, probably the wettest part of Kenya. For those isolated farmers their nearest railhead was Londiani – once mooted as the future capital of a combined Kenya and Uganda Colony, until the two went their separate ways. The distance from Londiani to the farming centre of the Uasin Gishu, Eldoret, was exactly 64 miles (102 kms) and for years that was what the settlers called it – "Sixty-four."

Preceding pages: Mixed goods train climbs one of the spirals on the steep ascent to the Timboroa Summit at 9,136 feet (2784m) on the line linking Mombasa with Kampala, built between 1926 and 1931.

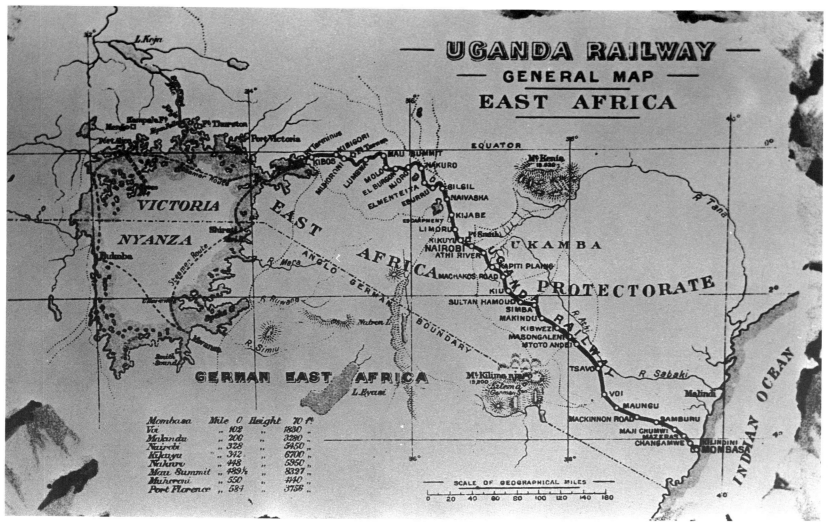

Above: Pre-First World War map of the original Uganda Railway with the line terminating at Kisumu — shown only as 'Rly Terminus'. In the 1914-18 War the line between Mackinnon Road and Makindu came under attack by mounted German patrols, but suffered little damage.

Above: Goods pile-up in the main goods yard at Kampala shows how great was the demand for rail freight during the 1930s after the opening of the Nile bridge at Jinja.

Right: Launch of the 'Sybil' at Kisumu in 1904. With her sister ship, 'Winifred', she opened up Lake Victoria to trade and continued in service for a remarkable 63 years.

Opposite: Uganda Railways passenger train crosses the White Nile where the river leaves Lake Victoria, Jinja.

Above: '56 Class' Garratt hauling EAR passenger train across the White Nile at Jinja where it leaves Lake Victoria on its long journey to the Mediterranean. Such was the challenge of bridging this fast-flowing section of the river, it took two years to complete the final link between Kampala and Mombasa.

The technical considerations were clearly compelling in favour of the direct line to Uganda following a separate but parallel route out of Nakuru, ascending the Rift Valley "wall" near Eldama Ravine. Yet there was a strong body of opinion which favoured a new extension branching off the Kisumu line after Mau Summit, which would reach the Uasin Gishu plateau among a thickly-forested but badly-broken ridge. This, the argument went, would not only be slightly shorter but obviously would also save much money in materials and labour on the construction of a second ascent out of the Rift.

In response, the technical experts and their many supporters pointed out that to carry the heavy traffic expected from Uganda, major improvements would have to be carried out to the original Kisumu line, including strengthening the track, rebuilding some viaducts and re-aligning stretches to eliminate the very sharp curves. This, they reckoned, would almost equal the cost of a completely new heavy-duty railway from Nakuru on to Uganda.

So much acrimony was generated over this issue that, at one time, the Kenya authorities banned any discussion of it in the Legislative Council. There were even vague hints that Lord Delamere, for instance, stood to benefit from a substantial increase in the value of his land that lay between the two parallel lines, if built. Others pointed out that another land developer, Colonel Ewart Grogan, who earlier had been granted large timber concessions in the areas of Eldama Ravine and Maji Mzuri, would also profit from the alignment passing through or near his timberland. Grogan, incidentally, was fortunate in owning 50 acres (20.2 ha) of valuable waterfrontage right where the new Kilindini deepwater berths were to be constructed at Mombasa and there might have been more foundation in the story that Grogan had asked for a vast tract of land on the Uasin Gishu in recognition of allowing the railway to pass through the timber area at Maji Mzuri.

In the end, the technical argument won the day and by 1925 the new line was snaking its way up a new alignment on the western side of the Rift Valley, by a tortuous route but manageable gradient, past Timboroa, just north of the Equator, where the railway reached its highest point of 9,135 feet (2,785 m). This was now the highest railway in the British Empire and the record still holds today for the Commonwealth.

By then, criticism of the new railway extension was coming from a new quarter. Farmers and businessmen in Uganda, of all races, were united in their objections to the fact that the railway management was "pandering" to the white settlers of Kenya – to the detriment of Uganda.

These critics held that freight rates on the railway had been deliberately weighted in favour of Kenya settlers and their produce, while the Uganda customers had to pay higher rates. What was worse, they complained, was the fact that all the revenue earned by the Uganda Railway from the time it began making a profit went straight into the coffers of the Kenya Treasury – despite the fact that most of the profits earned by the railway had come from cotton grown in Uganda. Especially vocal were the European and Asian plantation owners who alleged that the effect of these rail policies was to make Uganda's development subordinate to Kenya's. Opposing the construction of the railway into the Uasin Gishu plateau to serve the White settlers, the Uganda planters argued that the line could only be financed by further increases in the already high freight rates for non-settler agricultural produce.

Tempers became frayed, at times at the cost of common sense. In the Kenya Legislative Assembly, for instance, some settler representatives objected to plans for the rail extension into Uganda, ignoring the fact that revenue from the Ugandan traffic would be essential in maintaining subsidised freight rates and building new feeder lines for the benefit of settlers in Kenya.

Above: The gradient up the western wall of the Rift to Mau Summit rises 3,000 feet (914m) in only 40 miles (64kms) — through thick forest and small farms.

Amid all the rancour and bickering, the contractors pressed on westwards across the plateau where the going was some of the easiest they had encountered along the difficult route. The contract called for the completion of the line as far as Turbo, beyond the expanding settlement of Eldoret. It required fresh legislation to authorise any further extension of the line towards Uganda, and it took a motion by the Uganda members of the Inter-Colonial Railway Council to get things moving in that direction.

Once the railway had passed Eldoret, plans were made for a branch railway line running north to the rich and fertile area of Trans-Nzoia with a terminus at Kitale. Irked by news of yet another extension to serve white settler interests in Kenya, the Uganda members' motion was very frankly worded: "Whereas the Uasin Gishu branch line with rail head at Turbo is of no utility to the Uganda Protectorate, the Uganda Members of this council desire to record an emphatic protest against the charge of interest

Opposite: Goods train crossing curved viaduct in the rich farmlands around Molo on the Kisumu line.

and sinking fund and loss on working expenses of this branch being borne on the Uganda Railway estimates, and can only acquiesce in such a procedure on the distinct understanding that the Government of Kenya gives a definite undertaking to make the necessary financial arrangements in order to continue this line to the Uganda frontier with the least possible delay. The Uganda Members of Council believe that by such extension only can this branch line become a paying proposition within a reasonable period."

Beyond the Turbo railhead lay two physical obstacles which were to prove very costly to surmount, but in their determination to see the railway actually reach the source of the Nile, the British Government gave every encouragement to the Railway management to press ahead. At the same time, true to form, they were still very sparing with the cash.

However the problem of financing railway construction, once inside Uganda, was eventually solved when the Empire Cotton Fund provided a substantial contribution as part of its effort to stimulate increased production of cotton in the colonies.

Bridging the Nzoia River at Broderick's Falls was a simple operation and beyond that, across the border into Uganda, the going was fairly easy until the construction gangs reached the deep "finger" of Lake Kioga stretching south to M'pologama and down towards Lake Victoria. Like much of Lake Kioga, this terrain was more swamp than lake, and meant that much time and effort had to be spent on building substantial earthworks to form a causeway approach to a bridge. Due to the very unstable bed of the swamp, large cylinders had to be sunk, to act as piers for laying the bridge foundations.

Platelaying gangs started work on the 184 mile (294 kms) segment from both ends early in 1927, one operating westwards from the Tororo side and the other in the opposite direction from M'Bulamuti. This was the most convenient point for a junction on the existing Busoga Railway.

The entire work timetable had been contingent on the prompt delivery of rails and sleepers, plus other building material on the western side of the swamp. The plan was to ship all this stock from Kisumu across Lake Victoria to Jinja and then move it over the railway as it progressed eastwards from M'Bulamuti.

Labour problems intervened at the same time as the lake steamers were overwhelmed with other commercial cargoes. The railway engineers had been expecting the building materials to reach the other side of the swamp in the shape of ready-laid track. However, the situation was that by the deadline at the end of 1927, the rails and sleepers still lay stacked on the wharf at Kisumu awaiting shipment to Jinja.

Opposite: Exterior of Kampala Railway Station.

With the whole timetable in jeopardy, desperate measures were needed, and so a new road was hacked out of the virgin, tsetse-infested Busoga Forest for a distance of 70 miles (112 kms) from Mjanji. This was a tiny port on Lake Victoria, just over the border from Kenya, and the road was built to provide access to the western edge of the troublesome swamp, so that the track-laying could go ahead independently of the swamp-bridging operation which had also been delayed – in this case by very heavy rains.

By then work had already started on the new Uganda Railway extension. Because of the complicated swamp-crossing and other delays, construction costs eventually increased to about £7,000 a mile, but this was still much less than the £16,700 a mile charged by private contractors for the 142 mile (228 kms) stretch up out of the Rift Valley and across the Uasin Gishu Plateau.

Above: Uganda Railways' train bound for Kampala after leaving the border station of Tororo and its bell-shaped rock on the gradual descent to Lake Victoria at Jinja.

Opposite: Looking down on the western end of Kampala railway station as a train prepares to leave.

Left: Crowded main platform at Kampala railway station.

Left: Passengers and one of the many colourful station market stalls.

*Above: Twin diesel locomotives double-head a
passenger train about to leave Kampala for Kasese, in
the foothills of the Ruwenzoris, the fabled 'Mountains
of the Moon'.*

Above: Derelict '24 Class' steam loco rusts in overgrown yard at Tororo, its East African Railways livery a fading tribute to a failed alliance.

Ten months behind schedule, the railhead reached the eastern edge of the swamp at M'polongama, but another 15 months elapsed before the final section to M'Bulamuti was officially opened. By then, of course, trains coming from the east were able to travel all the way to Jinja over the now-incorporated Busoga Railway.

The line from the Indian Ocean at Mombasa, and across the floor of the Great Rift Valley and up through the Kenya Highlands had finally reached its ultimate goal – the source of the Nile. But to bridge that roaring torrent as it gushed out of the Lake required a major engineering achievement that took from 1929 until 1931.

The completion of the huge steel structure which arched above the Ripon Falls was marked by a formal opening ceremony, combined with the opening of the rail extension to Kampala. Presiding was Sir Edward Grigg, then the Governor of Kenya, but also the High Commissioner for both Kenya and Uganda. In his speech, he had somewhat fulsome praise for the economic manner in which the Railway's General Manager, Christian Felling, had supervised the building of the "Uganda Extension".

Above: Rows of spare bogies above a disused inspection pit in Tororo yard.

Reflecting the historical significance of the occasion Sir Edward said that while they had been talking of the railway line to Jinja as "an engineering and organising feat…these railwaymen here in Africa are not railwaymen only, they are really bearers and guarantors of our civilisation which is based upon the railway, and could not survive for long without it."

After pointing out that railways were as vital to the British Empire in Africa as roads were to the Romans in ancient Britain, Sir Edward said that the results of the Uganda Railway project started 30 years ago had "exceeded the wildest dream of its originators". Then – obviously thinking more of Kenya than its neighbour – the Kenya Governor went on to refer to the beauty and fertility of the Kenya Highlands and the great benefit which had been brought to the area by the railway: "It has been responsible also for the fact that we have been able to prove and establish economic crops over a fertile country which until its advent had absolutely no external trade. Cotton, coffee, sisal, maize and wheat – all these things have been brought here by European pioneers and all these things have been established simply because the railway has been built. Without the railway, none of these valuable crops could have been established here for a day."

The railway official on whom praise was so lavishly bestowed did not survive long after that ceremony on the banks of the Nile. Only eight months later he died from malaria, just weeks after he was dubbed Sir Christian Felling. He had been unable to take quinine, but had stayed on in spite of the danger to his health to see the job through, ignoring all medical advice that another bout of malaria would prove fatal.

Although the railway had finally reached the Nile's source, the river that poured out of Lake Victoria was no puny stream, but a steady torrent which required a bridge of high engineering standard to span it. The task was a daunting one and because of this and more pressing priorities, the railway authorities had already decided that plate-laying should first go ahead on the other arm of the "Uganda Extension", which branched off at Tororo to the northwest.

Realising that the Nile Bridge at Jinja would take several years to complete, the rail link to Kampala was left in abeyance. Not only would this connect Uganda's main town to the Railway, but also its capital, Entebbe, although, of course, these were already served by the Lake steamer from Kisumu. In any event, before the tracks were laid down, it was considered necessary to clear away much of the thick forest that covered the route and was a source of sleeping sickness attacking humans.

There was also another important consideration which occupied the attention of the railway management at the time – the question of whether or not the rails should eventually be pushed ahead westward into the Congo. Many British officials were then obsessed with the idea of "capturing" for the Uganda Railway the bulk of the traffic from the numerous mines opened in the north-eastern corner of the Congo. This had already influenced the decision to introduce the steamer route on Lake Albert, starting a service from Butiaba to two Congolese lake ports

130

which was essentially a "feeler" towards more permanent links with the mineral-rich neighbour across the water.

The fact that much of the machinery for these mining ventures had been brought up from Mombasa by the railway encouraged the planners in Nairobi to expect that the eventual outcome would be bulky and profitable return cargoes of mineral ores *en route* to Mombasa for shipment overseas.

Another consideration was a warning from economists that the Kenya-Uganda Railway – as it was called from 1926 onwards after it crossed into Uganda proper – should not depend entirely on the revenue derived from agricultural produce on the "down" traffic to the coast. They urged that everything should be done either to start mining operations in Kenya and Uganda, or persuade the Belgian authorities to ship out minerals from the eastern Congo through Mombasa.

Surveys had already established that the most practical rail route from Kampala into the Congo would be through Mubende and then south below the Ruwenzori Mountains. Construction costs had even been worked out at the fairly reasonable rate of £7,000 a mile, (1.6 kms) which, with extra rolling stock, would amount to about £2 million.

The Railways General Manager even went to Brussels in the hope of getting a firm commitment from the Belgian Government. But, though they showed interest, no concrete assurances were forthcoming that the line to Mombasa would be used as the principal outlet for the mineral exports from the Congo. Pessimism began to creep in after that, compounded by the disappointing performance of the Central Line in Tanganyika, which had been expected to carry the vast copper traffic from the Katanga mines of the Congo through Kigoma and out from the port of Dar-es-Salaam. Instead, the bulk of the freight was diverted via the Benguela Railway to Atlantic ports.

One obvious drawback of the Tanganyika outlet had been the fact that the Congo's railway system was compatible with the 3ft 6inch gauge (1.06 m) of the Southern African system, but not with the East African metre gauge. The end result was that all immediate plans for further extending the "Way to the West" were shelved, and the newly-built station at Kampala remained the end of the line for another two decades.

However, there was no such delay on the northern branch of the "Uganda Extension," where construction continued from Tororo to Mbale and on past Mount Elgon's foothills to veer north-west into the blooming cotton fields of Soroti and the Teso country. This was indicative of the priorities of the age. Cotton was the all-important cargo for the railway to carry out of Uganda and contributed the bulk of the revenue.

But the so-called "Sunbeam Period" in East Africa came to an end in the 1930's with the onset of the "Great Depression." For the railway it meant that almost no further development work took place for more than 20 years. In Uganda the line was halted at Soroti and this stretch of the northern branch did not reach Lira until 1962. Completion of the remaining segments was then rapid, with the service to Gulu opened in 1963 and to the terminus at Pakwach, on the White Nile, the following year.

Initially the Egyptian Government had negotiated with Uganda to construct a dam across the river at Pakwach. But when this did not materialise, there was no longer any urgency for a rail link, since the cotton-growing region across the river in West Nile, centred on Arua, was already well-served by the the steamer link from Lake Albert. It was only with the completion of the railway to Pakwach in 1964 that the steamers plying Lakes Albert and Kioga became superfluous and were finally withdrawn. Today, without her engines and fittings, the rusting hulk of "Robert Coryndon" lies at Butiaba, a sad memento of the bygone age of the Nile steamers.

The extension of Uganda's southern branch line beyond Kampala was spared the delays and disappointments that dogged the northern Pakwach route and by 1953 had pushed ahead as far as Mityana. Instead of passing through Mubende, it was routed along the Katonga Channel to skirt the northern boundary of Ankole District. It then made a steep descent of almost 3,000 feet (914m) in the last 30 miles (48 kms) down to the Lake George flats. The terminus at Kasese was eventually reached in 1956.

The final inducement to build this line almost to the Congo border was the opening of the Kilembe copper mine in the Ruwenzori foothills. An ore smelter had been built at Jinja and for years the Western extension carried the copper for smelting at Jinja before its export through Mombasa.

The most notable feature of the line west of Kampala was the ingenious engineering works needed to cope with the steep drop into the western fork of the Great Rift Valley. As at the outset of the line, just over a thousand miles (1,600 kms) behind and half a century before, a spiral rail configuration had to be built to deal with the gradient.

Over the passage of time, since the construction work began in 1951, the railway's impact on the country and people of western Uganda had decreased significantly. This was mainly the result of a rapid expansion of road transport and the fact that lorries provided stiff competition for the railways with regard to goods traffic by the 1950s. Even so, although the lorries had the advantage of speedy delivery, the railway consistently proved the cheaper alternative – especially when more realistic tariffs for freight transport on the line were introduced.

6 THE OLD AND PICTURESQUE LAKE STEAMERS

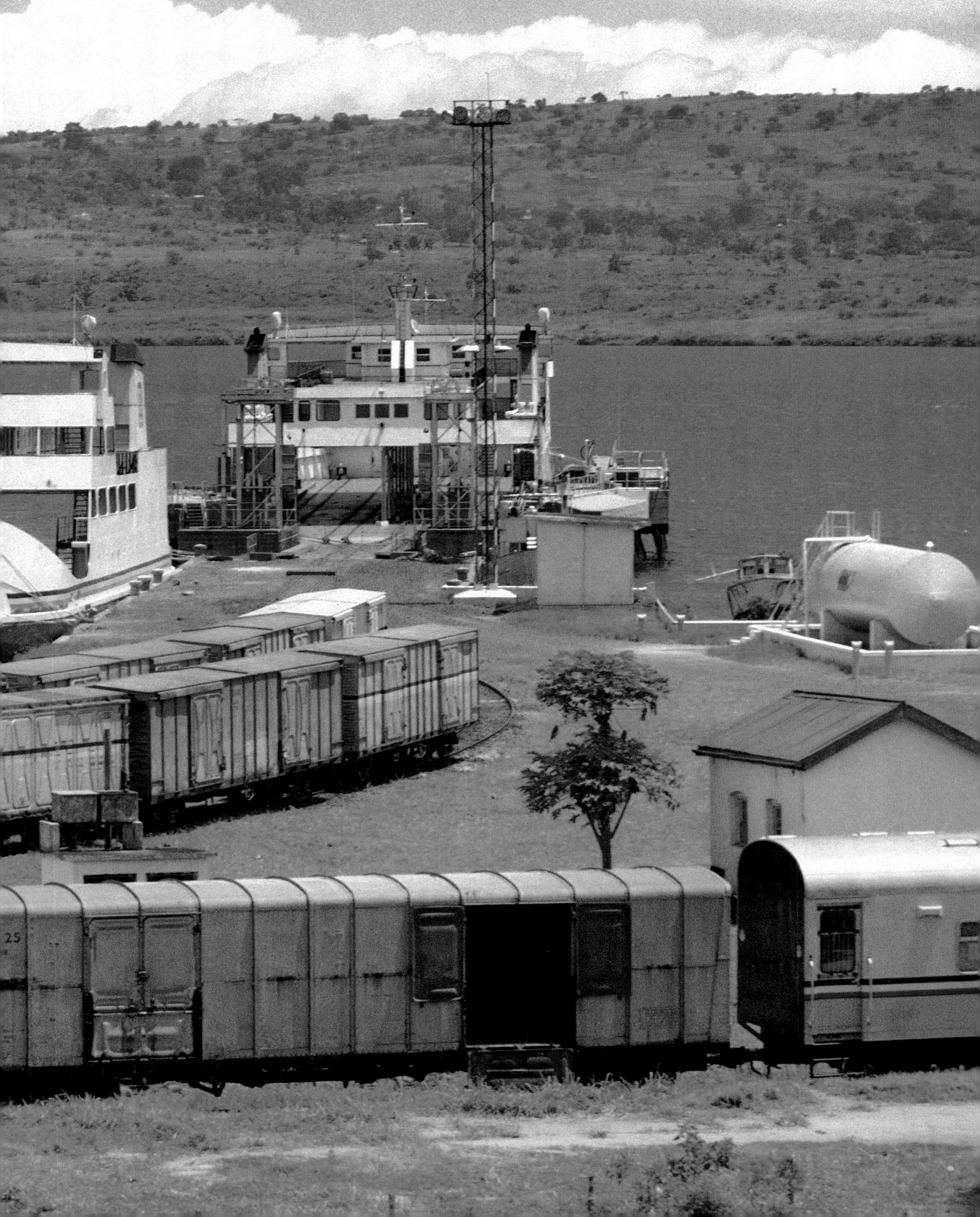

After Winston Churchill returned from his visit to East Africa as Under-Secretary of State for the Colonies in 1907, he wrote in his book 'My African Journey' how impressed he had been with the new Uganda Railway. He called it "one of the most romantic and wonderful railways in the world".

But the young Churchill was not enamoured with the White settlers he met in Nairobi and did not hold out much promise for the Kenya Colony-in-the-making, as he saw it then. To him, Uganda seemed to have far better prospects. Once back in Britain, his advice to colleagues at the Colonial Office was to "concentrate on Uganda".

"We already spend on East Africa and on the needs of the white settlers, more revenue than the whole of Uganda; and yet the prospect is not so bright. Already more than half the traffic which passes down the railway to Mombasa comes from beyond the lake, yet scarcely any money has been spent on Uganda," he pointed out.

In fact, Churchill saw the need for making maximum use of the many inland waterways which Uganda possessed and wrote in 'My African Journey': "The Uganda Railway is already doing what it was never expected within any reasonable period to do, it is paying its way…Projected solely as a political railway to reach Uganda and secure British dominance upon the Upper Nile, it has already achieved a commercial value…And this is but the beginning, and an imperfect beginning, for at present the line is only a trunk without its necessary limbs and feeders, without its deepwater head at Kilindini, without its full tail of steamers on the lake: above all without its normal and necessary extension to the Albert Nyanza."

The lake's "tail of steamers" was only a short tail then, but was due to grow fairly soon. With his uncanny insight into the future, Churchill also saw the need for a steamer link on Lake Albert. At that time the only vessels were those plying on Lake Victoria from Port Florence (later to be re-named Kisumu). They consisted of the 'Winifred' and the 'Sybil', both of which were operating a weekly service to Entebbe and back. From Entebbe, a steam tug, the 'Percy Anderson', which had been brought up from the coast, hauled a line of barges to Munyonyo, which served as the nearest port for Kampala town until Port Bell was developed later.

The 70 ton 'William Mackinnon' was too small to be of much use once the rail construction work had been completed. But the 'Clement Hill', named after a previous railway manager, proved a great asset to the lake "fleet" when it arrived in 1906. Her elegant lines were more suitable for a luxury yacht than for a workhorse in the heart of Africa. Although displacing 1,100 tons, she was of a much shallower draught than the 700-tonners 'Winifred' and 'Sybil', and was far more manoeuvrable when approaching the shallows of Kisumu. One year later, the 'Nyanza', a vessel just slightly larger than the 'Clement Hill' was launched.

Preceding pages: Newest rail ferries on Lake Victoria, the 'Kaawa' and the 'Kaawa Trader', were assembled in the early 1980s at Port Bell and are based at Jinja. Each carries more than 20 rail wagons on a twice-weekly service between Jinja and Mwanza, Tanzania, mainly loaded with export coffee which is railed to Dar es Salaam port over the Central Line.

Top: The German-built "Graf von Goetzen" in the Kigoma shipyard before launching in 1914. After only two years service on Lake Tanganyika, she was scuttled by the Germans as they withdrew in the face of the British Army advance.

Top right: After lying on the bed of the lake for several years, the "Graf von Goetzen" was refloated by the British and eventually put back into service in 1927 under her new name "Liemba". She is still operating on Lake Tanganyika.

Above: Gala 1947 welcome at Mwanza, Tanzania, during the maiden voyage of the MV 'Victoria', the first motor vessel to sail on Lake Victoria.

Right: The 'Grant', last of the three stern-wheelers which plied Lake Kioga, Uganda. Together with 'Stanley' and 'Speke' she formed a vital link in the 'Nile Route' — along which passengers could once travel all the way from Cairo to East Africa using a combination of train, ship and road transport along the length of the Nile.

136

No ships were operating on other Uganda lakes at the time of Winston Churchill's visit, but his comments exerted great influence on the railway management. His keen foresight can be seen in his historic prediction about the potential of the Nile at Jinja, when he confidently said: "It would be perfectly easy to harness the whole river and let the Nile begin its long and beneficient journey to the sea by leaping through a turbine." This was followed by another example of prescience when, back in Britain again, Churchill spoke of the enormous potential for cotton-growing possessed by the lands around the shores of Lake Kioga. This is a stretch of clear water bounded by thick papyrus growth along the shores, but the lake also has an intricate array of arms penetrating into the tribal lands of Busoga, Bukedi and even Teso, as well as Bunyoro in the north-west.

Although Kioga appeared quite unlike the other lakes in the region, the railway surveyors realised that this vast watery swamp had a 250 mile (400 kms) shoreline from which steamers could transport cotton and other marketable produce once a railway link could connect the lake with the pier at Kisumu.

Above: Before 1961 the route around Lake Victoria was operated jointly by the "Usoga" and the "Rusinga", but they took five days, as compared to 48 hours taken by the much faster "Victoria". The "Usoga" is seen here at Kisumu behind a Short Solent flying-boat of Imperial Airways, which regularly landed at Kisumu in the '50s.

Above: "Kamongo", one of the smaller ships plying Lake Victoria casts off from Kisumu Pier on a short voyage across the Winam Gulf to Kendu Bay.

Right: On the bridge of the "Kamongo" as it moves off from Kisumu Pier.

138

Above: "Kamongo" en route for Kendu Bay from Kisumu.

Largely as a result of Churchill's prodding, this railway soon took shape under the name of 'The Busoga Railway', albeit only a 57.5 mile (92 kms) stretch of metre-gauge track to begin with, running more or less parallel with the Victoria Nile, from Jinja to Kikundu. However, this terminus was soon found to be unsuitable as a steamer anchorage because of the river's swift current, so the line was pushed a few miles north to Namasagali, which proved a much better site for a steamer base.

Even before the Busoga Railway was completed, Lake Kioga had its first paddle steamer. The 'Speke' was the first of several "stern wheelers" which all resembled typical Mississippi steamboats of that same era. The 'Speke' began operating in 1910 but delays in bringing in track-laying material held up completion of the railway until 1913.

The original plan had been to build a line running directly to Lake Albert, reaching its shore either at the southern end, or at Butiaba, near the northern end of the lake. Both plans were rejected in favour of a rail-road-and-ship route, of which the Busoga Railway was stage one and the 'Speke' on Lake Kioga, stage two. After crossing the lake and negotiating the channels cut through the papyrus and other weeds, the 'Speke' docked at Masindi Port. From there, Albion cars were later introduced to span the land gap between Lake Kioga and Lake Albert at Butiaba.

The man who had first advocated the all-rail route to Lake Albert from Entebbe or Port Bell was a Major A.G.Stevenson, a great visionary. In recommending such a route, he wrote that a railway going to the southern extremity of Lake Albert could then be extended across the Semliki River "probably to the Congo, or even across Africa". Such were the wide horizons of men in that Imperialistic era.

But those with their eyes firmly fixed on the ground ahead were more swayed by the immediate advantages which Lake Kioga offered as a main waterway, as well as affording easy access to the cotton-growing areas – perhaps even to the foot hills of Mount Elgon and the Kenya border country.

At that time cotton was proving a great "money-spinner" for Uganda growers and the railway management was anxious to cater to the traffic this generated all the way to the port of Mombasa. But, in spite of cotton's potential export revenue, many farmers refused to grow it unless they could be assured of a nearby market where they could sell it. Some were quite adamant that unless such a market was less than two days' journey for porters carrying cotton bales on their heads, they would not grow the crop at all.

The British administrators at that time had little patience with such people, judging from a statement by the Chief British Commissioner at Entebbe. Writing in his annual report for 1903, Sir James Hayes-Sadler stated: "The great difficulty is to get natives to cultivate the right kind (of crops), and in sufficient quantities. They live under such easy conditions as regards food that there has hitherto been no necessity, and but little inducement, for exertion. In this I have great hopes for the hut tax, which obliges those who cannot pay in cash to do a month's work for the Government, and if, as I trust, Uganda becomes a producing country on a large scale, it will be largely due to the effects of this measure…When once the people see that it is easier to bring a load of produce for sale to the merchants than do a month's work on buildings and roads, and that there is easy money to be made, the inducement to extend cultivation will follow."

Several "ports" were created along the lake's swampy shoreline and to do this many channels had to be opened up through the tangled vegetation, or "sudd", which hindered navigation. There was a plan to open up a channel to neighbouring Lake Salisbury and the Teso country but wiser counsels prevailed, fearing that the difference in lake levels might cause problems. During the years of the First World War, Lake Kioga was to cause many headaches for ships' captains. While Lake Victoria had fallen on several occasions, the level of Lake Kioga as well as the Victoria Nile at Namasagali, rose alarmingly more than 12 feet (four metres), flooding all approach roads and, in some cases, even submerging the piers. Fortunately, little capital had been spent on these supporting facilities and on storage buildings so the damage for those operating the ships was not so much costly as inconvenient.

Below: The first two rail ferries on Lake Victoria "Umoja", and her sister ship "Uhuru", went into service in 1966, operating between Kisumu, Port Bell and Jinja in Uganda, and Mwanza in Tanzania. They are diesel-powered, with 800 horse-power V-8 engines, and a shallow draught of only 8ft 8ins (2.6m).

Eventually three ships were plying the waters of Lake Kioga, for after the tug, the 'Speke', pioneered the waterway, another stern wheeler, the 'Stanley', entered the service in 1913, carrying both passengers and cargo. The 'Speke' mainly handled the cotton traffic with barges in tow. The two of them gave outstanding service under very difficult conditions until the burden was shared with a third vessel, the 'Grant' in 1925.

A year before that, in January 1924, the Uganda Railway management took over the steamer service which the Uganda Government had been operating on nearby Lake Albert. This "fleet" was pitifully small, consisting of a 17-year-old paddle steamer, the 'Samuel Baker', and a steam launch, the 'Livingstone'. These two vessels opened up the lake which, at this point, formed the international frontier between Uganda and the Congo.

Lake Albert is fed by two rivers. The Semliki flows in at the southern end after traversing the fringes of the Ituri Forest and the foothills of the Ruwenzori Mountains ('the Mountains of the Moon'), and the Victoria Nile enters at the northern end, after passing through Lake Kioga and over the Karuma and Murchison Falls.

Although this river system helped to spark off the idea in Europe of a great inland waterway in Central Africa, neither of the rivers are navigable, except for a mere 25 miles (49 kms) of the Victoria Nile between Murchison Falls and Lake Albert. However, the river flowing out of Lake Albert, known then as the Albert Nile and now simply as the beginning of the White Nile, is much wider and navigable for some distance as far as the Sudan border.

At the start of the steamer service on the lake, the 'Samuel Baker' forged the first international route to the Congolese ports of Mahagi and Kasenyi, while the 'Livingstone' nosed her way down the White Nile to Pakwach, Rhino Camp and as far as Nimule, the border post with the Sudan. From then on, rapids barrred the way to Juba.

It was obvious to the Railway management that if the maximum use were to be made of this waterway, new and properly designed vessels would be required for negotiating the Nile's many sandbanks and to stand up to the sudden and fierce squalls frequently encountered on Lake Albert. In 1927 the stern wheeler 'Lugard 1' was launched on the lake and served the Nile route well until she was replaced in 1947 by 'Lugard II' after which the older vessel was used mainly for accommodating passengers.

The 'Samuel Baker' had a badly-needed refit in 1924 to enable her to continue plying the lake route, and then her replacement arrived in 1930 in the shape of a handsome and powerful new steamer, the 'Robert Coryndon', named after the popular former Governor. One of the final duties of the 'Samuel Baker' was to carry the British Prince of Wales across the Lake in 1928 after visiting the Murchison Falls. The 'Livingstone', in semi-retirement, was used mainly to carry tourists and hunting parties.

While the small fleet of ships on Lake Kioga and Lake Albert and the Nile did much to open up that part of Uganda for agricultural development by giving access to world markets for cotton and other commodities, these vessels were also to become world-famous as a vital link in the Nile steamer route which started in Cairo. Using a succession of ships, trains and the occasional bus, this route laboriously worked its way

south through the "sudd" of the southern Sudan into Uganda and ended at the shores of Lake Victoria. In its heyday this route earned a reputation in travel lore as romantic as that of the Orient Express and the Trans-Siberian Railway. It was a journey embarked on only by those with time to spare and a liking for a leisurely pace. Today, the Nile steamer route no longer operates south of Juba. With the opening of the rail extension to Pakwach in 1964, the steamers were all withdrawn from service on that stretch of the route.

On Lake Victoria, however, the story has taken a different course and this vast expanse of water measuring 26,560 square miles (68,800 square kms), is still busy with steamers and diesel powered craft criss-crossing its surface, carrying passengers and produce of every kind for the markets of East Africa and beyond. Few of the old-timers are still in service and some, like the stately 'Clement Hill' and the 'Winifred', were consigned in 1936 to watery graves when they were ignominiously scuttled at Kisumu to provide a breakwater against the rough waters that now and then rise in fury on the lake. The 'Sybil' was retired in 1936 and of the sister ships, 'Rusinga' and 'Usoga', which went into service just before the outbreak of the First World War, the former was withdrawn in 1966 and the latter was given a reprieve for a few more years.

Above: Passengers disembarking at the marine wharf of the Kenya Railways at Kisumu with other vessels in the background including the diesel rail ferry 'Uhuru' at far end of pier.

In place of the old maritime ghosts which still haunt the lake waters, handsome, powerful new ships keep the old route going, but at a much faster pace. Whereas the "Usoga" used to circumnavigate the Lake in a five-day dawdle, the 1,500 ton m.v. 'Victoria's' twin 'Caterpillar' 1150 hp diesels speed her round the circuit in 24 hours. The 'Victoria' was launched in 1961 and the later acquisitions arrived in 1966. These were the train ferries, the 1,180 ton sister ships 'Uhuru' and 'Umoja', which at over 300 feet (91.5 m) were the longest vessels on any of the East African lakes. Two more train ferries, the 'Kawa' and the 'Kawa Trader', each with a load capacity of 21 wagons, came into service with Uganda Railways at Jinja by the mid-1980s – assembled with Belgium help at Port Bell. They ply between Jinja and the Tanzanian port of Mwanza.

The vessel with the most chequered career of all the old East African steamers never sailed the waters of Lake Victoria or the Uganda lakes. She is the 'Liemba', a "phoenix" if there ever was one in the shape of a ship. She began life in 1914 as the 'Graf Von Goetzen' when she was ceremoniously launched into the deep waters of Lake Tanganyika at the inland terminus of the *"Deutsche Ost Afrika Mittellandbahn"* (Central Line) at Kigoma, the only large ship to be based on the eastern side of this 360 mile (576 kms) long stretch of water. The war was just about to start and Tanganyika, under German rule, found itself in the war-zone, facing the British to the north, and the Belgians to the west.

Just as some of the British-built vessels on Lake Victoria were put into war service as a "naval squadron", so was the sole German ship on Lake Tanganyika. Instead of being used to carry goods to and from the Belgian territories to the west and north of Kigoma, the 'Graf Von Goetzen' was armed with a powerful naval gun which menaced all enemy craft on the lake. A film featuring this vessel was eventually made under the title 'The African Queen', featuring Katherine Hepburn and Humphrey Bogart.

She was scuttled outside Kigoma in 1916 as the Belgians were advancing on von Lettow's forces, and lay in shallow water until she was eventually salvaged in 1924. With typical German thoroughness, her engines had been carefully preserved ashore and so the British, who by then had been given trusteeship rights over Tanganyika, overhauled the ship after her long years underwater. With her old engines refitted, the 'Graf Von Goetzen' was re-commissioned under a new name, the 'Liemba'.

Remarkable to relate, the 'Liemba' is still plying up and down the length of Africa's longest and deepest lake, having been in operation continuously since 1927, with the exception of a lapse when she exchanged her original German engines for modern diesels. With no restrictions on the draught in a lake so deep as Lake Tanganyika, she has a tonnage of 1,575 and a draught of nine feet (2.74m) whereas the maximum limit possible on Lake Victoria is 8ft 6 inches (2.62m). She remains the largest of all the East African lake vessels and her weekly run takes her from Bujumbura in Burundi, at the northern end of Lake Tanganyika, past several ports on the Zairean shore and her Kigoma base, then down as far south as the Zambian port of Mpulungu.

Together with some Zairean ships, the 'Liemba' still keeps trade going between Eastern Zaire, through the port of Kalemie (formerly Albertville) and via the Central Line from Kigoma to Dar es Salaam and the sea. This sturdy veteran is still in reasonable shape in spite of her wartime ordeal.

146

Although the Germans were comparative latecomers to the African colonial scene, their activities in East Africa at the turn of the 19th Century set a cracking pace for the older-established colonial powers to match. Indeed, it is doubtful whether the British "Lunatic Line" to Lake Victoria would ever have materialised from the realms of fantasy had it not been for Germany's own dedication to railway construction as the most immediate means to open up the African hinterland.

The German acquisition of a "sphere of influence" in East Africa closely paralleled the tactics and strategies of their chief colonial rivals, the British. They relied upon private enterprise in the early stages of their "scramble for Africa", in preference to direct Government involvement, only later resorting to State intervention when private investors shied away from the prospect of poor economic returns. The Germans more than compensated for their lack of experience in the colonial stakes by a single-minded determination to stamp their mark of effective occupation on the East African hinterland.

At the outset, it was a young man called Carl Peters who took the initiative by founding the Society for German Colonisation. From then on, the unfolding of Germany's Imperial ambitions in East Africa followed a breakneck course of treaty-signing, in direct negotiations with rival African tribal rulers, as well as outright annexation, all of which resembled a form of diplomatic "blitzkrieg". And yet, by the time it came to turning the gains of such field-agents as Peters into concrete colonial possessions, the Germans found their scope of activity restricted to a wide swathe of territory lying between present-day Mozambique and Kenya that later came to be known as Tanganyika.

The first European physically to set foot in the fertile highlands of East Africa was a German explorer, Dr Gustav Fischer, who had been commissioned by the Hamburg Geographical Society in 1882 to find a route from Mount Kilimanjaro to Lake Baringo. By the following year, Fischer had reached the Great Rift Valley, one year ahead of his better-known rival from Britain, Joseph Thomson. But Fischer was forced to turn back at Naivasha, in present-day Kenya, after being confronted by hostile Maasai warriors. He later reported that he had been most impressed with the area around Mount Kilimanjaro as being "best adapted for European settlement".

When Carl Peters, posing as an electrician and using a false name, later canoed up the Wami River to sign his first batch of treaties with the chiefs in the Usagara region south of Kilimanjaro, Dr Fischer commented favourably on Germany's new territorial acquisitions. He pointed out that Peters had secured for Germany the most strategic part of East Africa, astride the main Arab caravan routes from Zanzibar to the inland lakes.

Later, under the terms of the Brussels Agreement between Britain, France and Germany in 1890, the German sphere of influence in East Africa was recognized as centering upon these old-established caravan trails running south of Mount Kilimanjaro.

Preceding pages: Quarry train hauled by a '62 Class' diesel of Kenya Railways descends into the Rift Valley.

Below: The Central Line in Tanzania linking Dar es Salaam with Lake Tanganyika at Kigoma took seven years to build, reaching its western terminus only a few months before the war broke out in 1914. Although less mountainous than the Uganda Railway route, the Central Line was much longer and traversed swampy and difficult terrain. Africans formed the construction gangs throughout.

Below: Several very narrow gauge railways were built in Tanganyika in the 19th Century to give access to mountainous areas. This Mingoyo military railway was still in operation during the British occupation of German East Africa in 1918. British nurses pose for a photograph beside the quaint engine.

Above: Ceremonial reception on the Central Line as the first train draws into Kigoma in February 1914 — after a journey of 774 miles (1,238 kms) from Dar es Salaam.

Above right: One of the lighter '52 Class' Garratt articulated locomotives used during the post-war period on the Tanganyika Railways.

Right: H.M. Armoured Train "Simba" was built at the Railway Workshops in Nairobi, which provided many items for the British military after the First World War started. This train guarded the main railway to Mombasa against frequent German sabotage attempts.

Above: Tabora 'roundhouse' on Tanzania's Central Line is unique in East African railway systems. On the turntable in 1950 was a '20 Class' locomotive — one of four built in India for service in East Africa.

Left: Ingenious improvisation helped mount this Central Line bridge on its piers near Kigoma. Built on pontoons, the huge span was raised when the Malagarasi River came into flood then floated downstream where it was lowered into place.

Carl Peters found himself obliged to forsake the northerly Tana River route to Lake Victoria, as it now lay squarely within the British sphere. Not one to be so easily upstaged, Peters arranged for himself to be appointed Imperial German High Commissioner for the Kilimanjaro Region in the newly-declared German East Africa Protectorate in 1891. In this key position he was at last ideally placed to set about transforming his hard-won paper treaties with local chiefs into the nuts and bolts of effective physical occupation and economic development. And what better way for opening up the hinterland than the cold steel incursion of a railway line?

From the time of his earliest trail-blazing exploits into the African interior in the 1880s, Peters had cherished the firm conviction that railway construction would prove the best method for putting the long-established traders on Zanzibar out of business.

Largely due to his influence in 1887, the German East Africa Company had already commissioned a surveyor by the name of Von Hacke, to undertake a preliminary survey for a railway from Dar es Salaam to Morogoro. In Peters' grand design, Morogoro would serve as the inland junction from which branch lines would extend northwards to the Kilimanjaro highlands and westwards to the Great Lakes – Victoria and Tanganyika.

But this earliest of all railway surveys in East Africa had to be abandoned before completion, when a red-bearded slave merchant named Bushiri led a widespread revolt against German occupation along the entire length of the German East Africa coastline. Military reinforcements had to be brought in by the Germans to put down the Bushiri Revolt, and it was not until four years later, in 1891, that further railway surveys could safely be embarked upon.

The next survey explored the possibilities of a line running north from Dar es Salaam to the former slave port of Bagamoyo. It was envisaged that this line should then branch inland up the valley of the River Ruvu. This surveying expedition was financed by a group of South German bankers and was also covered by a guaranteed loan from the German Government, which had by now signed a contract with the German East Africa Company for the exploitation of all unoccupied land within nine miles (15 kms) on either side of the proposed railway lines running inland from the coast. Further conflict between the new German colonists and resentful African tribes soon broke out in central and southern parts of the Protectorate, which again put a stop to any immediate railway construction from Dar es Salaam.

However, in his northern headquarters at Moshi, at the base of Mount Kilimanjaro, Carl Peters would brook no opposition to the advancement of his colonial enterprise. Faced with a local uprising among the Chagga tribe, Peters used ferociously punitive measures to crush that rebellion. The relative tranquility of Peters' Kilimanjaro domain attracted the attention of the German railway builders at a time when the rest of

Below: Footplate view of the unusual rock formation ahead of a 1950s "down" steam train from Mwanza to Dar es Salaam soon after leaving the Lake Victoria port.

German East Africa was being devastated by widespread insurrection. A route was suggested for a railway from the northern port of Tanga to Moshi, passing through the fertile Usambara district, where the German East Africa Company had begun to establish the first plantations, mainly of rubber and coffee. A meeting was convened in 1891 of well-known German explorers and African administrators who generally agreed that the Tanga Line represented the most viable option for railway construction until the other parts of German East Africa had been pacified. The most vocal opponent of this proposed northern line was a director of the German East Africa Company William Oechelhaeuser, who advocated the importance of immediately striking out for the inland lakes along a Central Line (*"Mittelland bahn"*), running directly inland from Dar es Salaam.

But the renowned geographer and explorer, Dr O. Baumann, countered Oechelhaeuser's suggestion, maintaining that the Tanga-Moshi Line could itself serve as an eventual jumping off point for later extensions to Lake Victoria and Lake Tanganyika, but only after peace had been restored to the warring hinterland. In the meantime, argued Baumann, the proposed Northern Line could help stimulate investment for productive development and encourage the immigration of German settlers.

Baumann's argument won the day and in June 1891, the German East Africa Company (the *Deutsche Ost Afrikanische Gesellschaft*) submitted a memorandum to the Imperial German Government on the planned construction of an *"Usambara Bahn"*, and its possible extension to Tabora and Lake Tanganyika, with a branch line running from Tabora to Lake Victoria. With the consent of Chancellor von Caprivi, the company then set up a subsidiary for railway and port construction, called the *"Eisenbahn Gesellschaft fuer Deutsch Ost Afrika"* ("Usambara Line"). Its first undertaking was to be the building of a new port at Tanga, and a metre-gauge railway inland to Korogwe, a distance of about 50 miles (80 kms)

Under the terms of its Imperial Charter, granted at the end of 1891, the company guaranteed that the line would be opened for traffic at least as far as Muheza within four years and as far as Korogwe within 20 years! This ultra-cautious forecast no doubt was dictated by the shortage of money available to the company at the time – its initial capital was limited to two million marks. Construction estimates and completion timetables had to be drawn up before any surveys could be carried out. At this time plans for the rival British line from Mombasa were still held up by Parliamentary wrangling in London, so the element of full-scale competition had not yet emerged.

A pessimistic note was struck early on by the Governor of German East Africa, von Soden, who predicted in a despatch concerning the line's prospects that unless the company was backed by sufficient Imperial finance it would go bankrupt "in the shortest possible time".

152

Another omimous factor was the unexpected delay in preparatory survey work caused by an amazing foul-up at Tanga port. When the first team of German engineers was landed there by ship, their surveying instruments were left aboard and taken on to Dar es Salaam. The surveyors had to cool their heels in Tanga until the end of the year, waiting for their equipment to be transported back up the coast on the next northbound vessel.

Finally, the survey party began work on mapping out the route to Korogwe, but the Germans failed to take adequate precautions against the local health hazards and they were soon stricken with malaria. The leader was replaced by his deputy, who in turn was obliged to hand over to a third man, who also went down with fever, so that all three were forced to return to Germany prematurely.

Then, early in 1892, the first construction experts – mostly recruited from the German State Railway system – arrived in Tanga aboard the SS "Kaiser".

They set about erecting temporary quarters for themselves and built the first workshops and a primitive jetty for landing the railway materials. In the aftermath of the Bushiri Revolt, they were faced with an acute shortage of labour and had to bring in migrant workers recruited in Mozambique. Soon they ran into the same difficulties in obtaining local building materials as were to face the British across the border in Mombasa. For instance, sleepers cut from nearby forests proved unsuitable and had to be replaced with steel ones shipped from Europe.

Meanwhile the survey parties pressed ahead, relying on hastily improvised reconnaissance methods, and in June 1892 they had reached Bombuera. Only later was it discovered that their makeshift surveying techniques had frequently missed the best alignments. Commenting on this unsatisfactory work, the Traffic Manager of the Tanga Line, Herr E. Kuhlwein, said later: "Considering this was the first railway ever to be constructed in a German colony, it is not surprising that mistakes were made and many miscalculations occurred."

Eventually, nearly two years after the arrival of the first German surveyors, Chief Engineer Bernhardt landed at Tanga in 1893 to supervise the track-laying. It took him a full year to complete the line between the port and the railway station.

By the end of 1895 the railhead had reached Muheza, 25 miles (40 kms) from the coast. When this initial section of the track was officially opened on 1 April, 1896, only half the line had been properly ballasted because of shortage of local stone.

Poor alignment had forced Bernhardt to use very cumbersome techniques for overcoming steep gradients. Near Ngomeni he built a "double switchback" to deal with one particularly difficult incline – which, as it later turned out, was entirely unnecessary. For many years these initial mistakes were to prove great obstacles to the smooth and economic running of traffic on the Tanga Line.

Governor von Soden's gloomy prediction appeared to have been realised at the end of 1895 when the railway company ran out of funds and construction ground to a halt. The District Commisioner at Tanga lamented in a despatch to his superiors in Dar es Salaam: "Only one train a week runs, on Saturdays, from Tanga to Muheza and back. All construction work has come to a standstill. Although the preparatory work for the extension of the line to Korogwe has been completed, the company's funds have been exhausted. Part of the jetty at Tanga, constructed in 1892, has collapsed and nothing has been done to repair the damage."

When the German Governor, Herr von Liebert, inspected the completed section of the line in 1897, he was so shocked by its state of disrepair that he wrote to the Imperial German Foreign Office in Berlin: "The railway construction is, and remains, a stain on the colony. The risk of bad work by private contractors must not be taken again. It was child's play for the Englishmen to build the 200 kilometres railway through the arid steppe from Mombasa to Voi. Germany, on the contrary, has hopelessly compromised and ridiculed herself by giving up after 43 kilometres. We owe it to the German name that the new work does not result in failure. I, therefore, recommend that the extension be carried out by the Reich."

The Governor's dramatic appeal was to prove a turning point in the fortunes of the railway. In 1898, a new survey was carried out by Master Builder and Engineer, Herr Todsen, who prepared a detailed estimate for extending the line to Korogwe. He suggested rails that were heavier – 40 pounds per square yard as compared to the 31 pound rails previously used – and also suggested that the line's gauge be narrowed to two feet (60 cms).

Then, on 7 April, 1899, after a two-year lull in construction, the railway company's assets were finally acquired by the German Government in the name of the Reich, for 1.5 million marks. Fresh funds were pumped in and a new management appointed. The labour force was greatly enlarged and work hived off to a number of competing sub-contractors. Among them were Greek railway experts who had gained an international reputation for their work on the recently-completed Baghdad Railway.

Previously inadequate medical facilities were much improved and steps were at last taken to reduce the serious toll from malaria and other prevalent diseases encountered by workers along the line. Engineers and other expatriates were required to wear hats in order to lessen the effects of the harsh sunlight. The strain of railway construction in Africa's harsh tropical climate showed up in the heavy consumption of alcohol among German and other foreign workers. After visiting the railhead, the Medical Officer at Tanga commented on the large number of empty spirit bottles he had seen scattered in the vicinity of the camp site. "These bottles," he wrote, "showed that the inhabitants of these camps tried to compensate, in their own fashion, for the hard lives they have to lead."

Above: One of the Central Line's '26 Class' steam locomotives entering the shed area at the Lake Victoria terminus, Mwanza.

In March 1901, the Reichstag approved a grant of 2.25 million marks for the Korogwe extension, and a year later a further one million was voted. But there was still reluctance to grant funds for any railway extension beyond Korogwe – even though the survey teams had by now pushed as far as Mombo.

Heavy rains continued to hamper the construction teams and delayed the opening of the Muheza-Korogwe line until March 1902. The rate of construction had slowed down at this stage and by the end of the year there were again serious doubts over the chances of the railway ever reaching the Kilimanjaro Region.

Governor von Goetzen anxiously lobbied his political masters in Berlin, pointing out that many German farmers and sisal-growers had taken up offers in the highlands in anticipation of the railway's arrival and the opening up of export opportunities.

Germany's most experienced "old Africa hand", Dr Carl Peters, himself added an influential voice to the rising public clamour back home in Germany over the stalled rail construction: "Germany's railway project has come to grief at the hands of the Centre Party," he wrote in 1902.

Meanwhile, faced with renewed shortages of labour in the Usambara Region, the German authorities contacted their British counterparts in Mombasa to ask whether there was any chance of obtaining the services of experienced Indian railway workers, who had recently completed the Mombasa-Lake Victoria line in an incredibly short time. It seems that very few of them took up the German offer.

So acute were the labour shortages on the route beyond Korogwe that the Railway Administration asked Governor von Goetzen to impose forced labour on the local people. The Governor rejected these appeals. He had received a report from the military commander in Tabora confirming that three-quarters of the railway work force had "deserted" at Korogwe because of the poor rates of pay compared to those being offered on nearby plantations being opened up by settlers. Von Goetzen's advice to the railway authorities was to increase their workers' wages.

Competition from the plantation-owners did not stop at poaching the railway's labourers: in June, 1904, an export company formed to exploit the rich forests of the Eastern Usambaras began work on its own *private* railway to serve the newly-erected sawmill located at the foot of the mountains. This 2ft 6in gauge (75 cm) line ran over very rough ground for 15 miles (24 kms) and joined up with the main line just beyond Muheza. Eventually completed in 1910, this "freelance" branch-line greatly shortened the existing approach route to the eastern Usambara mountain range and for many years served as the main access to the Germans' prestigious Agricultural Research Station at Amani.

Whether spurred on by the arrival of this private-enterprise line, or in response to the Governor's complaints about their conditions of employment, the railway company embarked on a vigorous new phase in 1904. A new contractor was hired – Lenz & Co – with a chief engineer, Herr Nissen, to replace the previous Chief Engineer. Adequate financial and technical resources were at last forthcoming and work on the route skirting the Usambaras suddenly speeded up. A key bridge over the Pangani River was completed with no hitches, and the new Korogwe-Mombo section was officially opened in February 1905 by Prince Adalbert of Prussia.

At this point it had taken 12 years to build only 80 miles (129 kms) of mainline track. But with the arrival on the scene of Lenz & Co., far more rigorous construction and maintenance standards were introduced. On April 6, 1905 the company reached an agreement with the Imperial Government on the formation of a subsidiary to be known as the German Colonial Railway Construction and Administration Company (*Deutsche Kolonial Eisenbahn Bau und Betriebe Gesellschaft*). Armed with four million marks of new capital, the subsidiary assumed direct responsibility for operations along the Tanga Line. One of its first moves was to carry out a detailed inspection of work already completed – and its findings provided grim reading.

The entire line showed serious lack of repair and defects in available rolling stock. "Engine No.1 is in a very bad state...Engine No.2 is in the workshop for heavy repairs...The axles of Engine No.3 are worn out...Engine No.4 is in fair state...Engine No.5 is in urgent need of repairs...Engine No.6, in spite of recent repairs, needs attention again...Engine No.7 can no longer be used on the line, but supplies steam for the machines in the workshop. Out of seven engines, only two are railworthy. These still working on the Tanga-Mombo Line often have to receive running repairs between stations."

The inspection report drew attention to the fact that some European railwaymen also owned plantations along the route, or worked part-time for local plantation-owners, as well as for the railways.

However, under its dynamic new management, the Tanga Railway soon began to forge ahead and make up for lost time. By July 1907 construction was under way on the extension from Mombo to Buiko, skirting the foothills of the Usambara Mountains. So encouraging was this new rate of progress that Under-Secretary of State von Lindequist recommended additional assistance for opening up the northern highlands of German East Africa. As a result, the Reichstag granted 12.25 million marks to extend the railway as far as Moshi.

The successful completion of the final stage of track up to the Kilimanjaro foothills can be attributed mostly to the arrival of a young Dutch engineer, Leon Kooyker, who had walked all the way to German East Africa from South Africa. He was an able and painstaking surveyor whose skilful reconnaissance work on the Moshi extension was a considerable improvement on the previous ill-judged choice of routes and alignments. (Later, he was to prove a valuable asset to the builders of the Central Line from Dar es Salaam to Kigoma.)

Germany's Northern Line from the Indian Ocean to Mount Kilimanjaro was finally opened to traffic on 7 February, 1912, with an impressive display of pomp and ceremony. By then, the line had been renamed the *Ost-Afrikanische Nordbahn*.

It was not until May 1914, with war-clouds looming over Europe and the rest of the world, that funds were approved for the final extension to Arusha. A German plan, drawn up at this time, showed their intention was eventually to push the railway on directly through Arusha to skirt the southern slopes of Ngorongoro Crater, past Lake Eyasi and across the Serengeti Plain to Lake Victoria at Mwanza.

In the two years it operated under German control prior to the outbreak of the First World War, the Tanga to Moshi Line was plagued by a series of ludicrous wrangles between railway officials and the colonial authorities. District Commissioners strongly objected to one regulation which obliged them to obtain permits for venturing on railway property, even on official duty. Absenteeism by engine-drivers, even on Christmas Day, was viewed by the railway administration almost as though it was an act of sedition against the state.

A persistent campaign against the railway was waged by the editor of a local paper and his highly-critical reports were picked up by papers in Germany. As it turned out, however, it was discovered that the editor's criticisms sprang from the fact that he had missed the train. He had been drinking in a nearby bar and the train-driver had pulled out of the station without waiting for him to finish!

Below: Steam locos in the shed at the 'roundhouse' at Tabora — an important junction on Tanzania's Central Line.

Above: The most recent railway development in Tanzania has been the Chinese-built Tazara line known as "The Great Uhuru Railway" from Dar es Salaam to the Zambian copperbelt. It was designed to provide land locked Zambia with an alternative route to the sea.

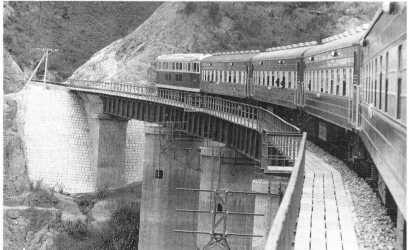

Above: Opened in 1976 "The Great Uhuru Railway" has many substantial earthworks and bridges, but its engines — diesels from the very start — lacked power to haul trains laden with heavy copper ingots from Zambia to Tanzania.

THE CENTRAL LINE (The 'Mittelland Bahn')

The German-built Central Line from Dar es Salaam to Kigoma was later described by a British Governor, during the period when Tanganyika was a League of Nations trust territory as the country's "spinal cord".
Although the first survey teams began reconnaissance work out of Dar es Salaam as early as 1894, construction did not get underway until ten years later with the formation of the Ost Afrikanische Eisenbahn Gesellschaft, and Berlin's grant of 21 million marks for capital costs.

In the intervening years the central and southern parts of German East Africa were riven by a series of bloody conflicts between the colonial authorities and defiant tribal groups doggedly resisting the imposition of full-scale German rule. Putting down this persistent insurgency which culminated in the Maji Maji uprising of 1894-6, was a much more urgent priority for the German administration than competing with the British in a railway race to the Great Lakes of Central Africa.

At the turn of the century when the Colonial Council in Berlin finally approved construction of the Central Line to the lakes, the go-ahead was justified as part of what it termed "a railway policy fully conscious of the aim to counter the competition of neighbouring colonies".

The main contractor for the Central Line was the Frankfurt- based company of Phillip Holzmann, which had recently completed the first section of the Baghdad Railway. Many of their officials were transferred directly to German East Africa from Baghdad in 1904. They ran into trouble soon after the railhead had moved a short distance from the coastal belt and encountered the vast flood-plain of the River Ruvu. In this area treacherous clays and sandstones were inundated with floodwaters every rainy season and required many more girder bridges, laid on far deeper foundations, than had been anticipated.

Like the British in the early stages of their Mombasa-Nairobi line, the Germans found few local sources of food for their labour force of Wanyamwezi workers and they had to import large quantities of rice from Bombay. But when the first stretch of track from Dar to Morogoro was opened at the end of 1907, the construction rate had reached 41 miles (67 kms) a year – a far healthier rate of progress than on the Tanga-Moshi Northern Line.

The railway's arrival at Morogoro coincided with the opening of a far more positive and vigorous phase in Germany's colonial policy. In the aftermath of the bloody Maji Maji rebellion, which had been put down with the assistance of troop reinforcements from German possessions in the Far East, the Imperial Government had set up a Colonial Department in Berlin, under the direction of a well-known banker and economist, Dr. Bernhard Dernburg. One of his first moves in 1906 had been to replace the Governor of German East Africa, Count von Goetzen, with Freiherr Rechenberg.

Above: Old E.A.R.&H. crest in use until the 1977 break-up of the East African Community. The red lion denotes Kenya, the giraffe Tanganyika (now Tanzania), and the crested crane Uganda.

Right: Exhibits in the Nairobi Railway Museum, where a wealth of history about Railway development in East Africa can be found.

The following year, Dr Dernburg himself sailed out to East Africa to conduct his own investigation of the economic potential of the area. He first disembarked at the British port of Mombasa and travelled up the Uganda Railway to Lake Victoria, before heading overland to Morogoro – just in time to meet the first German locomotive to steam into the newly-opened station.

While attending a celebratory banquet at a nearby hotel, Germany's new colonial overseer revealed far-reaching plans for the extension of the Central Line across German East Africa all the way to Lake Tanganyika. A loan of 80 million marks from the German Government to the railway company was announced, and this lavish assistance was generally taken to imply a virtual state take-over of the German East Africa Railway Company as a public utility.

Beyond Morogoro, controversy arose over the Dodoma route finally chosen by the survey team which ran far to the north of the alignment originally proposed, via Iringa and the fringes of the fertile Southern Highlands, then being settled by German colonists. Critics accused the authorities of sacrificing the colony's long term economic development for speed of construction to Lake Tanganyika. A Cologne newspaper in March 1907 said: "This Central Line has been for a long time the stepchild of railway planning in Africa. Obstacles of many kinds have been placed in its way."

One obstacle the railway experts could not overcome was the lack of suitable stone for ballast along the track. An attempt was made to use coral rock railed from the coast, but the tracklaying gangs found that it quickly pulverized and was of little practical use in binding the steel sleepers.

The line between Morogoro and Tabora followed the old slave route to the hinterland of the Great Lakes region. The only construction difficulty encountered on this section was the climb up the steep Rift Valley wall at Saranda, a gradient of 1 in 50.

The Reichstag was ready to approve the final extension of the Central Line from Tabora to Lake Tanganyika, at the end of 1911, but the railway authorities were still dithering over their choice of a final terminus on the lake shore. Alternative surveys had been aiming for Kigoma, Karema and Bismarckburg at the southern end of the lake. It was only when a comparatively cheap and technically efficient way of descending from the central plateau was discovered that Kigoma was decided upon as the most natural terminus. The Central Line reached Kigoma's well-protected harbour on 1 February, 1914, fourteen months ahead of schedule. This fast rate of progress in the latter stages of construction owed much to the introduction of a new mechanised method of platelaying.

Generally, the Central Line presented few engineering problems for German railway-builders, as compared to the Northern Line, running through fairly open and gently rolling woodland at an average altitude of 4,000 feet (1,220 m). Only during the torrential rainy seasons did the construction teams encounter any serious difficulty, having to throw up heavy embankments to carry the rails over the swollen flood plains of major rivers such as the Ruvu, Mkata, Nyahua and Malagarasi.

The most notable engineering feat along the route was the building of the bridge over the Malagarasi River on the final run down to Lake Tanganyika from Tabora. Here the Germans resorted to an ingenious technique for placing the bridge's huge 150 foot (45m) central girder in position: it was assembled on pontoons at low water and floated into place on the rising floodwaters.

Over the mostly arid stretches of the Central Plateau, transport of food and water for the work force presented the most serious drawback. To overcome this critical supply problem, Sikh and Punjabi contractors were employed to set up a special overland caravan-trail from the fertile Kilimanjaro region, using donkeys to carry food and even drinking water down to the work camps along the railhead.

The total cost of the Central Line was approximately 111 million marks. On the eve of the First World War, the line's rolling stock consisted of 63 engines (44 of them tank engines), 30 passenger coaches, 319 goods wagons, 29 water trucks, four mobile cranes, 39 derricks and 98 trolleys. The Central Line was an engineering "walkover" compared to the trials and tribulations of the Northern Line to Moshi. Yet, in the long run, the economic advantages of the line from Dar es Salaam to Kigoma never began to compare with those opened up by the Tanga-Moshi route.

Historical records show that the German authorities had all along regarded the Central Line as a "springboard" to the mineral-rich Congo, lying on the far side of Lake Tanganyika, then in the possession of the Belgians. The outbreak of the World War in 1914 and Germany's subsequent defeat put paid to its long-term ambitions of reaching any deeper into Africa's hinterland.

Throughout the German colonial period in Africa, plans were regularly mooted for building a third railway from the coast to the fertile Southern Highlands and Lake Nyasa (Malawi). The first survey teams sent out from Kilwa were halted by the outbreak of the Maji Maji Rebellion and when construction of the Central Line began to get underway in 1907, it was believed that the Southern Highlands would eventually be tapped by a branch line from this "spinal cord". A reconnaissance was carried out by Herr Denninger, senior engineer on the Baghdad Railway, who surveyed routes to the Iringa and Mbeya regions, and right through to the Rhodesian border and Lake Nyasa.

Denninger's detailed proposals would have involved building 1,250 miles (2,000 kms) of track through very difficult country at a cost of 360 million marks. His projected alignment called for several complicated "rack" sections. The scheme was eventually turned down after the railway authorities decided that the costs and construction problems would exceed the anticipated economic advantages of the line.

In the last few months before the outbreak of war, a detailed survey was also made for a metre-gauge railway to run from the southern port of Lindi through the Lukuledi valley to link up with navigable sections of the Rufiji River which formed the southern frontier with Portuguese East Africa (now Mozambique). Again this idea had to be abandoned because of hostilities. A reconnaissance was also made in 1915 into the possibilities of linking up the Central Line and the Northern Line, but by then the Germans were on their way out as an effective occupying power in East Africa and it was not for another half century that Tanganyika's two original railway lines were finally connected – at the dawn of independence in 1963. It was then possible for trains to go all the way from Dar es Salaam, via Moshi and Voi, to the Kenyan capital of Nairobi and then on through the great Rift Valley to Kampala and almost to the Congo (Zaire) border at Kasese.

Once the First World War ended and the situation in Tanganyika returned to normal in the 1920s, the British authorities, then with a League of Nations mandate to govern the territory, began to look at development priorities and make plans for new construction projects once the supply position had improved.

As far as the country's rail network was concerned, there was much to be done before Tanganyika could catch up with the progress already made by Kenya and Uganda. It was not until 1928 that Mwanza, the port at the southern end of Lake Victoria, was finally connected with the Central Line by an extension running north from Tabora. One year later Arusha became the final terminus of the Northern Line from Tanga, three whole decades having passed since the Germans started the line at the coast with the object of opening up Northern Tanganyika for agricultural development.

The decision to connect Mwanza to the Central Line and form a second rail link between Lake Victoria and the Indian Ocean in competition with the Uganda Railway to Mombasa came only after a major row had erupted within East Africa. It revived the long dormant differences between senior administrative officials in Kenya who were then mostly subservient to white settler pressures, and those in Tanganyika who saw their priorities in a different order.

The original plan had been to drive a railway line south from the Central Line, roughly following the old caravan route to Lake Nyasa (Malawi) and on into Nyasaland and Northern Rhodesia. Several surveys had been carried out and the one finally favoured would have branched off the Central Line at Dodoma, going due south to Iringa and giving access to the fertile Southern Highlands for settlement.

It was at this juncture that the major difference of opinion developed. Kenya, then politically dominated by white settler interests led by the voluble Lord Delamere, was toying with the concept of a so-called "Great White Dominion" spread across the face of Africa from Kenya down to Nyasaland and the Rhodesias.

The Kenya settlers saw Tanganyika as a major obstacle to fulfilling this "grand design" for settling white farmers in the temperate highlands throughout Eastern Africa. Lord Delamere had lobbied unceasingly over the years to have a policy for white settlement introduced into the country, similar to that in Kenya's "White Highlands", and he still hoped to convince the administrators in Tanganyika to back his plans.

As early as 1925, he had driven all the way down from Nairobi to Tukuyu, in the Southern Highlands of Tanganyika and one of the potential white settlement areas near Mbeya. It was a rough five-day drive over an unmade road, jocularly referred to at the time as "the Great North Road".

The purpose of his journey was to attend a meeting called specifically to bring the white settlers of the five countries (Kenya, Tanganyika, Nyasaland, and the Rhodesias) in closer touch with one another.

Preceding pages: Modern mixed goods train passing through rich farmlands around Emali, Machakos district. From its earliest days, the railway carried Kenya's farm produce to the coast for export. Today mineral exports and manufactured goods have joined the wagon-loads of tea, coffee, pyrethrum and canned fruit which make up much of the Kenya Railways' export tonnage.

Overleaf: For single-line working on East Africa's metre gauge tracks, the "tablet" system is still used. The hoop-like "tablet" is handed to an engine driver arriving at a station, permitting him to enter the next section. With only one "tablet" for each section, the system eliminates the risk of collisions through human error.

Right: Impressive array of heavy Garratt articulated locos at Nairobi engine sheds during the halcyon days of the East African Railways Corporation in the late 1950s. Largest was the '59 Class' with a tractive effort virtually double that of earlier models.

Right: Because they were lighter, the '60 Class' Garratts, made by 'Franco-Belge,' were used on branch lines, including that running north from Nairobi below the slopes of Mt Kenya and ending at Nanyuki.

Right: 'Baganda' one of the last orthodox 2-8-4 wheel arrangement locos to go into service in East Africa in 1955 before the articulated Garratts provided most of the motive power. These 'Tribal Class' engines served throughout the E.A.R.&H. system.

Delamere had already formed a company for the Tukuyu area, called "Colonists Limited", with capital provided by himself, Lord Egerton of Tatton, and others. It was a land agency with transport links to the nearest town, Iringa, 300 miles (480 kms) away.

Word soon got around that southern Tanganyika was to be a "second Kenya", and this started an exodus of white farmers from Kenya which was later joined by Germans, with similar hopes of acquiring farms on which to settle. Vital to these plans was the proposed rail link to Iringa and possibly further south to Mbeya and the north end of Lake Nyasa (Malawi), then into the north-east corner of Northern Rhodesia. This, the planners reckoned, would give Northern Rhodesia a much-needed outlet to the sea at Dar es Salaam.

The meeting of settlers at Tukuyu voted in favour of the rail route passing through the Southern Highlands, in preference to an alternative which would have run further to the east, ending on the eastern shore of Lake Nyasa (Malawi) without reaching Northern Rhodesia. Subsequently the highlands route was also approved by a conference of East African Governors.

Funds for the construction had already been made available as a result of a £10 million loan for transport in Tanganyika which had been recommended by a British Commission sent from Whitehall. Elated at the prospect of the new railway line being built and their bold gamble paying off, the settlers even began building a railway station at Iringa to receive the expected trains!

By this time Lord Delamere was being referred to in the Press in South Africa as "the Rhodes of East Africa", and he was busy working out details of the Federation he hoped would consolidate the Whites' permanent hold on East Africa.

But they had reckoned without the Governor of Tanganyika, then Sir Donald Cameron, who not only vetoed the plan for any White settlement in southern Tanganyika in 1926, but had the route of the proposed railway extension changed so that it headed in the opposite direction, going north from Tabora to Mwanza, instead of south from Dodoma to Iringa.

His action went directly against the decisions of the four other Governors, who all shared Kenya's fear that the Mwanza line would lead to unfair competition with the Uganda Railway. But they had been over-ruled by the Colonial Secretary in London, who in the end supported Cameron.

Opposite: Today just another bridge, but many died in getting the Uganda Railway across this river, the Tsavo, at the end of last century. A pair of man-eating lions terrorised the construction workers for months, killing at least 28 Indian labourers before the marauders could be hunted down and shot.

Above: Kanga, one of the few railway stations located inside a wildlife sanctuary, is a wayside halt in the vast Tsavo National Park.

Above: The old engine sheds.

Lord Delamere should not have been surprised at the turn of events, for he had already had an argument with Sir Donald Cameron during his visit in 1925. On that occasion, the Governor reminded His Lordship that Tanganyika was a mandated territory under League of Nations trusteeship and not a British possession like Kenya, where the disposal of land to whites had been part of official policy.

Cameron had gone even further at that time, making it clear to the Chief Secretary of Tanganyika in Dar es Salaam that he opposed any plan for a 'Great White Dominion'. Explaining why he was so strongly against it, Sir Donald said: "The trouble with your 'Great White Dominion' is that the gods saw fit to place a large and predominant proportion of Africans in these territories. We've no right to squeeze them out of here."

Above: Painter sprays the Kenya Railways livery onto refurbished passenger coaches at the Nairobi Railway Workshops.

For some time afterwards relations remained strained between Kenya and Tanganyika until the colonial administrators on both sides of the border began to realise that it would be in the best interests of East Africa to create some form of regional grouping which would directly benefit the three neighbours – Kenya, Tanganyika, and Uganda, together with Zanzibar which was then a separate unit, still ruled by a Sultan.

When the Second World War came to an end and a more liberal atmosphere prevailed after the return of East African troops from helping the Allied campaigns in North Africa and Burma, thoughts turned towards devising some form of closer union, as well as a greater autonomy for the African people in the colonies, (and in trusteeship territories such as Tanganyika).

Opposite: Skilled diesel engineers check out a '93 Class' loco over inspection pit in the Nairobi Railway Workshops.

Above: Sign-writer puts the finishing touches to the 'KR' — Kenya Railways — logo introduced soon after the break-up of the East African Community in 1977.

Below: Youngster waiting to watch the trains go by, rests on the protective casing over the signal wires.

Lengthy discussion dragged on until 1948 when a compromise was reached to form an East African High Commission which would oversee the creation of certain common services for the three mainland states. A Central Legislative Assembly would also be created, with its Members drawn from the constituent territories.

One of the first moves the Assembly made was to authorise the amalgamation of the railway systems, and exactly four months later the East African Railways and Harbours came into being. Writing later in her book, 'The Making of Tanganyika', Lady Judith Listowel described this action as "one of the greatest benefits the Assembly conferred on Tanganyika".

The amalgamated system brought a certain amount of standardisation and pooling, but the limiting factor remained the lack of any rail link between Tanganyika's Central Line and the northern network. This gap was eventually closed in 1963.

The heyday of the unified railway system operating throughout East Africa lasted just under three decades from 1948 to 1977, after which narrower nationalism superseded the wider regionalism of the earlier Pan-Africanist visionaries.

Above: Strange cargoes are carried by rail passengers on some trains. This woman from a rural area alights with a pair of gourds which serve as cheap but useful containers.

Above: Maasai elder perches on the side of a brake van — happy to cut short his long walk.

It was on 1 May, 1948, that the East African Railways and Harbours parastatal and regional organisation was formed, with the amalgamation of the Kenya Uganda Railway and Harbours (K.U.R.&H) and the Tanganyika Railway (T.R.) systems. The new regional network began operating over a combined area of 700,000 square miles (1.8 million square kms) with associated lake steamer and road transport services reaching out to places the railway could not serve.

At the peak of the E.A.R.& H.'s activity, the total rail mileage measured 3,669 miles (5,870 kms). In addition, the Inland Marine Service covered another 3,469 route miles (5,550 kms) and road services (mainly in Tanganyika) totalled 6,059 miles (3,787 kms).

Only in the middle of the period when the E.A.R.& H. was in "full bloom" did the northern and southern rail networks become linked up. In 1963, soon after Tanzania and Uganda had attained independence and on the eve of Kenya's own "Uhuru", Tanganyika's President Julius Nyerere officially opened the 117 mile (187 kms) link between the Northern (Tanga) Line and the Central Line at Makinyumba Station.

This made it possible for rail traffic to move from Dar es Salaam to Nairobi and beyond, through Kampala to Kasese in Western Uganda

Opposite: *Although there are motorised trolleys for track inspection, many gangs still operate with muscle-powered hand trolleys.*

below the "Mountains of the Moon". Within another year (1964) it was also possible to journey by rail from Pakwach, on the banks of the White Nile, to Kigoma on the shores of Lake Tanganyika, only a few miles from where Stanley had his first historic encounter with Livingstone at Ujiji.

By 1965, the hectic years of rail construction work were almost at an end. Since then there have been no major new works on railways in Kenya or Uganda. For some time it also seemed that the railway system in Tanzania would become subservient to road transport, with the improvement in that country's road network. Although a 24 mile (38 kms) stretch of line was built in 1965 from Mikumi to Kidatu to serve the fast-developing sugar-producing area in the Kilombero Valley, Tanganyika had otherwise just experienced the ignominy of a failed "groundnut scheme". This ended in the tearing up of many miles of track in 1963 which had been laid with high hopes only a few years previously.

Under a hastily-contrived and over-ambitious scheme, the British Government hoped to produce 600,000 tons of groundnuts over a three-year period to provide badly-needed oils and fats for the hungry nations of post-war Europe. A railway was built inland from the minor ports of Mtwara and Lindi in southern Tanganyika to open up the hinterland around Nachingwea and Masasi. Work continued from 1949 to 1958, while some 5,000 square miles (12,950 square kms) was being cleared of bush to make way for the groundnuts – until the entire project was abandoned and this remote area, together with another near Kongwa was allowed to sink back into obscurity. So ended the "Southern Province Railway".

Over the years great advances had been made in both locomotive design and the standard of rail travel. Corridor coaches were introduced in 1926 soon after the line from Mombasa reached Uganda. They proved a popular innovation, although it led eventually to the phasing out of the "dak bungalows" which had provided comfortable overnight accommodation for joining and departing passengers, as well as hearty meals for through travellers. The advent of dining cars merely transferred the wayside meals to on-board fare and the decor on the first and second class dining cars was luxurious in the extreme – almost a direct "steal" from the Orient Express. But on the line between Nakuru and Kisumu it was not until the 1960s that these dining cars were added because the sharp curves prevented the lengthy carriages from being operated. The last of the wayside meal services was provided by the bungalow at Lumbwa.

The motive power department of the Uganda railway, and later the Kenya Uganda Railway, experimented for many years with articulated engines to help overcome the handicaps imposed by the many steep gradients on much of the line. Their first attempts were with "Mallets", introduced back in 1913. Their performance was a disappointment, as the engines needed constant repairing and eventually had to be relegated to secondary duties and off the main line working.

The Germans in German East Africa earlier tried "Mallets" on both their Tanga and Central Lines, but they were much smaller and more compact. Most were deliberately destroyed by the German forces when they retreated from the British troops during the First World War, and long stretches of track were also torn up.

The biggest advance on the Kenya-Uganda system came in 1926 with the introduction of articulated locos of the Beyer-Garratt type, although a heavy 4-8-0 (Mikado-type) wheel arrangement engine of the "EB Class" was already doing good work on the construction phase of the railway in Uganda just before the "Garratts" arrived to begin regular haulage work. The "EBs" were improved later in 1928 with the addition of super-heated steam.

As metre-gauge engines were a rarity in Europe, but were in use over much of Asia, the East African Railways' management turned to the Far East and India for second-hand engines, or for "split-orders" in cases where other customers had made large orders, or had a surplus. A number of engines came from the Bengal-Assam Railway late in the 1920s, and others came to East Africa from Malaya and Burma.

The first "Garratts" to reach Mombasa came from railways in Indo-China. They had complicated (for that time) wheel arrangements of 4-8-2 + 2-8-4, and the first four were followed some years later with another 18 of an improved version, which served East Africa well for more than 35 years. All were coal-fired and, in comparison with the more orthodox locos operating on the Kenya Uganda Railway, they were much lighter, although larger.

Conversion from coal to oil began in 1947, but some of the engines on the remoter stretches of line continued to burn only wood for many years afterwards, especially in Western Uganda.

Preceding pages: Two of Kenya Railways modern diesel locomotives passing each other on main Mombasa-Nairobi line. Fifteen of the '92 Class' type were purchased from Canada in 1970 and a later batch, the '93 Class' — on right — from the United States in 1978.

Above: One of the few orthodox steam locos working in East Africa as the steam age drew to a close was 'Tsoto', a 'Tribal Class' engine with a 2-8-4 wheel arrangement here nearing Dagoretti on the outskirts of Nairobi.

The world's first 4-8-4 + 4-8-4 "Garratts" of the "57 Class" arrived in Kenya in 1939. They were much heavier, weighing 186 tons as against the 125 and 128 tons of the earlier "Garratts". Their 24 wheels were designed to spread the heavy load more evenly along the track so as to enable these locos to operate over tracks with fairly light trails.

Altogether 154 Beyer-Garratt articulated locomotives were put into service with the E.A.R.& H before steam was finally phased out by the end of the 1970s. Three of the last four classes to arrive were leviathans of the track, especially the 34 locos of the "59 Class", all of which had a pulling power of 83,350 lbs twice that of the earlier models of "Garratts". This type reverted to the 4-8-2 + 2-8-4 wheel arrangement and carried the names of East Africa's principal mountains. The "59 Class" were the most powerful metre-gauge locos in the world and became among the most photographed of all the E.A.R.& H. fleet, especially "Mount Gelai" with its maroon livery and gleaming brasswork, kept shining by the same devoted crew which had worked her for 16 years.

These "Garratts" regularly hauled the mail trains between Mombasa and Nairobi for many years until they were finally withdrawn in 1980 and 1981, to be entirely replaced by diesel locos from various countries including Britain, Canada and West Germany.

Steam locos over the years had caused many problems to the East African railway engineers, especially boiler troubles, due mainly to the chemicals in the water supply in more remote areas, and to the different types of fuel used. In some cases certain types of locomotives were used for purposes other than those for which they were designed, purely by force of local circumstance, and this considerably reduced their working lives.

Providing suitable and sufficient water for the thirsty engines of the bigger classes was particularly difficult on the long, dry sections of the Central Line in Tanganyika until the "30 Class" was introduced in 1955 with tenders which could carry 7,000 gallons (31,822 litres) of water.

Above: One of the '60 Class' light Garratt articulated locomotives nearing the end of its working life taking on water at Thika on the Nanyuki branch line. Made by the Franco-Belge Works, this class was introduced to East Africa in 1954. Their lighter weight made them ideal for working the branch lines. In its latter days the E.A.R.&H. system relied heavily on its three classes of Garratts for most of the heavy work — until the diesels took over completely in 1980.

Several of the early types of engines had amazing durability despite the arduous working conditions in East Africa. The 2-6-4s of the "10 Class" were in service for more than half a century, from 1914 right through to 1965, and the 31 locos of the "11 Class" built at the Lancashire plant of Britain's Vulcan Foundry Locomotive Company lasted all the way through from 1926 until their well-deserved "retirement" in 1967.

During the quarter-century from 1925 that the six engines of the "28 Class", built by the famous makers, Robert Stephenson & Co., had worked on the Kenya-Uganda Railway, they had all completed a million miles (1.6 million kms) and were immensely popular with the crews who worked them. They were still in service 10 years later, but after being switched from pulling passenger trains to hauling fast good trains, serious mechanical problems led to their withdrawal early in the 1960s.

Diesel locomotives were first tried out in Kenya in 1956, working the steep gradients of the mineral line descending down the Rift Valley to Lake Magadi. They were gradually integrated into the system after extensive trials, which at times produced the curious spectacle of an English Electric "1-Co-Co-1" working a "double-header" with a vintage "steamer" such as a 30-year-old "Class 28" loco.

Although there were the usual "teething troubles" and the old-timers among the drivers had to become accustomed to the novel form of traction, the diesels' light weight proved a blessing to the track maintenance crews. Compared with the 186 tons of the "59 Class" Garratt, the English Electric locos weighed 120 tons and a Canadian diesel only 98.5 tons.

Apart from the gradual changeover to the diesel locomotives, the most interesting development to take place on the E.A.R.& H. system was the introduction of rail ferries on Lake Victoria. Twin craft, the 'Uhuru' and 'Umoja', were put into service from Kisumu in 1966, with the necessary "roll-on, roll-off" facilities for wagons. They operated a regular service out of the Kenyan port to Mwanza and Jinja.

"THE GREAT UHURU RAILWAY"

The largest development on the railway scene in East Africa since the 1960s, however, has been the construction of the major rail link between East Africa and Central Africa, known as the "Great Uhuru Railway", or variously the "Tazara" or "Tanzam" Railway.

This 1,160-mile (1,860 kms) long track, built to 3ft 6inch (1.06 m) gauge, runs from the Tanzanian capital, Dar es Salaam, through the south-western part of the country to Kapiri Mposhi, in Zambia, linking up with the existing rail network of Southern Africa. It does not form part of the original, and larger, Tanganyika Railway system, and has its own governing body, the Tanzania-Zambia Railway Authority, jointly controlled by the two Governments.

Below: Brasswork gleaming, the well-known 'Mount Gelai', a 'Mountain Class' Garratt which was manned and maintained — in immaculate order — by the same footplate crew for more than a decade.

Below: Evening sun catches gleaming paintwork as it begins the long haul up to Nairobi.

The railway was built under a loan agreement between China and Tanganyika and Zambia, using local labour working with several thousand Chinese experts and artisans. The total cost of the construction, together with locomotives and rolling-stock, came to $230 million. The route traverses some very difficult country, especially in south-western Tanzania between Iringa and Mbeya, where there are very steep and high escarpments.

When the Tazara Railway opened in 1976, it filled the gap that had existed on the rail map of Africa ever since the authorities in German East Africa had abandoned their planned railway line to the south during the outbreak of the First World War. Expectations that the earlier German plans would be put into effect after the war, when Tanganyika was under a British mandate, also failed to materialise.

The over-riding argument for the building of the rail link between Tanzania and Zambia was the need for Zambia to export its copper ore to the outside world without having to depend on the South African ports and railway system. It finally provided land-locked Zambia (formerly Northern Rhodesia) with an alternative and more direct link route to the sea through another African state, instead of having to depend on South Africa.

This was the first railway line to be built from scratch in East Africa for use by diesel locomotives and steam was never used on this line. Although the engineering works are of a good standard and its concrete sleepers are an innovation for East Africa (wooden sleepers have been used only at points and on bridges) the railway has nevertheless suffered serious shortcomings. Its performance has become very erratic largely due to the frequent mechanical failures of the locomotives which are underpowered for the task they have to perform – hauling heavy freight trains over long distances and up some steep gradients. The railway has also been plagued with financial difficulties, compounded by the fact that two governments are jointly in control of the funds.

On several occasions in recent years, the railway has come to a complete halt because there has been no money to meet the fuel bills. At other times, shortages of wagons have been the problem, according to Tanzania,

Above: One of the 34 'Mountain Class' Garratts employed on the East African Railways network, 'Mount Nyiru', waiting in the Nairobi goods yard ready to draw out for the 300 mile (500 kms) run down to the Coast. These were the largest metre-gauge locomotives in the world and twice as powerful as any other engine in the region.

Above: No 3145, 'Wamia', last of 103 engines of the 'Tribal Class' 2-8-4s to go into service between 1951 and 1955. The complicated valve-gear is clearly visible as 'Wamia' draws out of Dagoretti hauling a goods train up the long incline to the edge of the Rift Valley Escarpment.

whereas Zambia blames slow working at the port of Dar es Salaam as the main bottleneck.

China has been asked to reschedule the loan repayments and has agreed to help rehabilitate the line. A further $150 million is being sought from the international community to help give the Tazara Railway a new lease of life. This would enable heavier loads to be carried over reconditioned track, reinforced with better ballasting, while new equipment for handling container traffic and other heavy loads is installed. Meanwhile, as a temporary measure, some locomotives from West Germany are to be used to supplement the ageing and underpowered Chinese engines.

The fact that Tanzania recently ratified the new Preferential Trade Agreement (PTA) for East and Central Africa gave a much-needed boost to the railway. In addition to more traffic from Zambia, assurances have been forthcoming from Malawi, Zimbabwe and Zaire that they would route more of their goods over this railway in future. (Malawi and Zimbabwe used to depend on their rail outlets to the sea through Mozambique, but guerrillas have recently destroyed parts of these routes, while Zaire and Zambia can no longer depend on the Benguela railway through Angola for a similar reason).

The most serious blow to the future development of the East African railways as a unified system came in 1977 with the break-up of the East African Community, and, with it, the common services it controlled, including the East African Railways Corporation (by then the Harbours had grown into a separate corporation).

All rail links and steamer services joining the three states were severed and have never been fully restored. Although after a seven-year period of non-cooperation a certain amount of working together was resumed, it amounted to little more than token co-operation and there is still no through working on the Kenya-Uganda sector of the railway from Mombasa. Kenya trains travel as far as the Malaba border station, and pasengers destined for stations in Uganda, including Kampala, must walk the short distance to the waiting Ugandan Railway train for the onward journey. Internal unrest has forced the closure of the routes to the west from time to time.

After years of rusting on the shores of Lake Victoria, the diesel steamer 'Victoria' is once more doing her rounds of the lake ports after an extensive overhaul, and the train ferries are also active. One new development has been Uganda's launching of its own train ferries which take Ugandan coffee and other produce across the lake to Mwanza and over the Central Line Railway to Dar es Salaam for shipment overseas. This is part of Uganda's current policy of reducing its dependence on Kenya for access to the sea. It is also a gesture of encouragement to Tanzania to press ahead with its long-range plans for extending the Northern Line from its present terminus at Arusha across the Serengeti Plains to Musoma, as an alternative and more accessible port for Uganda's exports.

Meanwhile, with the juggernauts of the roads having replaced the leviathans of the rail, the railways are facing stiff and direct competition from road transport roughly along the same routes. But the "ace" card still held by the railways is that their rates are cheaper and, as far as passenger traffic is concerned, trains are very much safer.

To keep up with the times, the Kenya Railways Corporation, which now operates over 1,656 route miles (2,650 kms), has equipped itself for the efficient handling of container traffic, with "inland container ports", including Nairobi, to cope both with rail and road traffic, or transhipment from one to the other.

While modernisation is a necessary corollary to a transport system approaching the 21st Century – there is now even a "Man-eaters Motel" overlooking the scene of the carnage in 1898 at the Tsavo River crossing – the trains which now run over that same old route of the Uganda Railway have not altogether lost their romantic image.

Although jetliners whisk travellers from Nairobi to Mombasa in an hour or so, and the drive takes little over five hours in a fast car, the 13-hour rail journey is still popular, and a "must" for those tourists who appreciate the old-world luxuries of the overnight Upper Class "sleeper".

There is still a lot to be said for the more leisurely tempo of the train

Above: A section of Kenya's former "Royal Train" was taken out of retirement to carry Queen Elizabeth II on her 1983 visit to Kenya. These special coaches went into service in 1922, and since then have carried several Royal personages and Heads of State.

Overleaf: Silhouetted against the Equatorial sky high above a mountain river at Maragua, a diesel-hauled goods train heads for Nanyuki.

Right: Queen Elizabeth alights from the Royal coach on arrival at Thika, followed by Kenya's Vice President Mwai Kibaki.

journey while dining in the dining cars, to the "clickety-click" sound of the rails. If it is one of the older types of car, the well-polished mahogany panels and the intimate glow from the table lamps more readily recall the long-gone Victorian age. On the spotless white table linen there can still be found the occasional table knife of sterling silver with the old "UR" initials on the handle, or maybe a cruet set with the "KUR" engraving, which was 'new' in 1926.

And then, after coffee or liqueur, it's off to bed in the made-up bunk of the day compartment, eventually to wake up to the rosy hues of dawn picking out the animals on the Athi Plains (if the train is heading up-country to Nairobi). Travelling in the other direction, the dawn light illuminates the tops of the coconut palms on the approach to Mombasa, where the great adventure all started – back in the 1890s.